*So the Word became human and
lived here on earth among us.
He was full of unfailing love and
faithfulness....*

(John 1:14 NLT)

Contents

Introduction

A BACKSTAGE PASS

If you want to encourage someone who has never read the Bible to begin reading it, then I would suggest that you direct him or her to the Gospel of John.

Certainly you could encourage them to start elsewhere in the Bible, because all of Scripture is inspired by God and has important truths and lessons for us as followers of Jesus. But a better place to begin would be John, simply because it was written so that an unbeliever might believe. I am so confident in the power of this Gospel that I think if a person would just say, "God, if You are real, reveal yourself to me," and then begin reading John's Gospel, that he or she can be transformed and believe. And many have.

There is another reason John's Gospel was written. It was so that we as believers might experience more of Christ's life in us. John 20:31 sums up for us the reason this Gospel was written: "But these are written that you may believe that Jesus is the

Christ, the Son of God, and that believing you may have life in His name." The word used here for "believing" speaks of a continual action. So John was saying that the more we believe, the more life we will experience.

Thus, John wrote this Gospel not only to convince the skeptic, but also to encourage the believer in the commitment he or she has already made.

John brought unique perspectives to his Gospel. In fact, 90 percent of the material found in the Gospel is not found in any of the other three. It is in John's Gospel that we hear the great "I am" statements of Christ: "I am the bread of life" (6:48); "I am the light of the world" (8:12; 9:5); "I am the good shepherd" (10:11, 14); "I am the resurrection and the life" (11:25); and of course, "I am the way, the truth, and the life" (14:6).

John stands apart from the other Gospels.

John had the unique advantage of having the other three Gospels before him when he wrote his Gospel. This brings us to the question, "Why four

Gospels?" Because each one was written from a unique perspective.

Matthew, also known as Levi, was a Jew. The Lord saw him sitting at the tax office and said, "Follow Me." And Matthew got up and followed Jesus. Therefore, Matthew, as a Jew, wrote his Gospel to fellow Jews to tell them that Jesus was the long-awaited Messiah of Israel.

Mark was not one of the twelve apostles. Many believe the Gospel that bears his name was actually dictated to him by the apostle Peter. Mark wrote in a breathless manner, almost in the way a reporter would write. Mark frequently used the words, "straightaway" and "immediately," indicating the quick pacing to his Gospel.

Luke was a physician. He wrote with meticulous detail and interviewed many of the people who were eyewitnesses to the ministry and life of the Lord. Like Mark, he was not an eyewitness himself. He obtained the information and recorded it in writing, doing so in a beautiful, even poetic, manner.

John stands apart from the other Gospels. First of all, it was written by an eyewitness, but not just any eyewitness. This eyewitness had a backstage pass, so to speak, to the ministry of Jesus. Remember that Peter, James, and John went with the Lord on a number of occasions when the other disciples did not. When Jesus was transfigured, Peter, James, and John were with Him.

Without a doubt, John was profoundly perceptive.

When He raised Jairus' daughter from the dead, it was Peter, James, and John who were there. When Jesus was experiencing His agony in the Garden of Gethsemane, again, He had taken Peter, James, and John with Him.

John was the brother of James. They were fishermen when they were called by Jesus to leave their nets, follow Him, and become fishers of men. John originally was a follower of John the Baptist, who one day pointed to Jesus and said, "Behold the Lamb of God!" From that moment on, John began to follow Jesus.

John had some amazing insights into the life and ministry of our Lord. He had a close relationship with Jesus. Often we will read in John's Gospel that he would lean his head on Jesus' chest. He was close enough to hear something the other disciples would not have heard, such as a whisper, or something Jesus might have said under His breath. Without a doubt, John was profoundly perceptive. He seemed to pick up on things when others did not.

Interestingly, he refers to himself in his own Gospel as, "the disciple whom Jesus loved." At first, this almost sounds boastful, as if to say, "Jesus loved me more than the rest." But that wasn't it at all. It was simply an acknowledgement of God's love for him. John would not boast of his love for God. Rather, he was boasting of God's love for him. And I like that. I would rather boast of God's love for me than my love for God, because my love for God can be so fickle sometimes. Yet God's love for me never changes. It is completely consistent.

In the pages ahead as we look into some of the earliest days of Jesus' ministry and how He responded to someone in need, to someone who was looking for answers, to someone who was hurting and empty, and to someone who was alone and without hope, my prayer is that you "may be able to comprehend with all the saints what is the width and length and depth and height—to know the love of Christ which passes knowledge"

(Eph. 3:18–19), and that along with John, you will be able to say, without a doubt, that you are a disciple whom Jesus loves.

1 WHEN HEAVEN CAME DOWN

Teachings from John's Gospel

In December 1956, a television game show called *To Tell the Truth* made its debut on CBS. The show featured three contestants who all claimed to be the same person. It was the job of a four-member celebrity panel to determine which contestant was telling the truth. The show always ended with that now-famous question, "Will the real _____ please stand up?" The outcome was always a big surprise.

Now imagine for a moment that you are a panelist on *To Tell the Truth*, and there are three contestants on the show claiming to be Jesus. It is your job to determine who the real Jesus is. The first contestant stands up. He has brownish-blonde, shoulder-length hair, and a short, well-trimmed, beard. He is not very muscular. In fact, he seems to be a little slight. But you notice his piercing blue eyes and the otherworldly expression on his face. He is holding a staff in one hand, and a lamb is

draped around his neck for good measure. So you
think, "He looks a lot like those pictures I've seen.
That is Jesus for sure!"

The next contestant stands up and says, "I am
Jesus." When he glances your way, he seems to
have this look of approval regarding who and what
you are. He seems completely nonjudgmental, and
more to the point, rather benign, even devoid of
conviction. You begin thinking about how this
Jesus might work well in your life. So you think,
"Maybe that's the real Jesus."

Then the third contestant stands up. Right away,
you notice that he is a stark contrast to the other
two. He is no shrinking violet, this contestant. He
appears to be strong, even masculine. At the same
time, there seems to be a tender quality about him.
As you look closer, you notice something else. He
radiates goodness. He even seems to be holy. And
suddenly you start feeling a little uncomfortable
about your life. You realize that you're not the
person you ought to be. There is something that
needs to change. But when you make eye contact
with him, instead of seeing rejection and condemnation in his eyes, you see love—not a watered-

down love like the other, but a sense of someone who loves with a real genuine affection and care. He makes you want to be a better person. He makes you want to change.

So which Jesus will you choose? Will you choose the stained-glass-window Jesus who looks the way you expect him to? Will you choose the benign Jesus who requires nothing and, for all practical purposes, will do nothing, because he is but a figment of your imagination? Or, will you choose the real Jesus of the Bible who loves you and yet challenges you to change? That is the Jesus before us in the Gospel of John. That is the Jesus who became flesh and walked among us.

Now, I don't know what Jesus looked like physically. I can only venture a guess. What is amazing to me is that John, the author of this Gospel we're about to explore and someone who spent a great deal of time with Jesus, did not even mention it in passing. It would appear that Jesus was rather ordinary in the way He looked. In speaking of the Messiah to come, the prophet Isaiah wrote, "He has no form or comeliness; and when we see Him, there is no beauty that we should desire Him" (Isaiah 53:1).

After the resurrection, Mary thought He was the gardener (see John 20:11–16). The two disciples on the road to Emmaus took Him to be an ordinary man (see Luke 24:13–27).

Certainly there is no passage that tells us Jesus walked around with a permanent halo. But what we do know from Scripture is that He was Jewish.

John was saying that we can have a relationship with God as significant as the one he had.

And in those days, this meant that he most likely would have had dark skin, dark hair, and dark eyes. So I seriously doubt that Jesus had wavy, sun-bleached, blonde hair and blue eyes. Now if you want to imagine Him that way, then that is your privilege.

But I find it interesting how, throughout history, various cultures have presented and interpreted Jesus' physical appearance. What I've noticed is that He changes with the times. In the paintings of Christ from the Renaissance period, He is dressed in the clothing of that day. In works from other periods, the current culture is reflected in the way that Jesus looks. Even in movies about Christ made in the 1950s, the actors who portrayed Jesus often had a matinee-idol look about them. The culture of the day influenced the way in which Christ was depicted. An exception, I think, is *The Passion of the Christ*, where Mel Gibson, with his meticulous attention to detail, historicity, and commitment to what the Bible actually says, captured something we have never quite seen before. It is almost as though the film transports the audience back in time. We get a sense of what it really must have been like.

A CREDIBLE WITNESS

What a thrill it would have been to walk and talk with Jesus, to hear His voice with our own ears, and to see His face with our own eyes. How many of us have wished we could have been one of the twelve disciples who had the privilege of listening to Him, speaking with Him, hearing the timber of His voice, and looking into His eyes? Yet it would appear that those days are gone, and we cannot have such a privilege. Or can we? According to John, who personally walked and talked with the

Lord during His earthly ministry, we can.
He wrote in his epistle of 1 John,

> *That which was from the beginning, which*
> *we have heard, which we have seen with our*
> *eyes, which we have looked upon, and our*
> *hands have handled, concerning the Word*
> *of life—the life was manifested, and we have*
> *seen, and bear witness, and declare to you*
> *that eternal life which was with the Father*
> *and was manifested to us—that which we*
> *have seen and heard we declare to you, that*
> *you also may have fellowship with us; and*
> *truly our fellowship is with the Father and*
> *with His Son Jesus Christ. (1 John 1:1–3)*

John was saying that we can have a relationship
with God as significant as the one he had. "We
walked with Him," John was saying. "We talked
with Him. We had that privilege. We spent prac-
tically every waking hour in His presence." The
phrase John used, "which we heard," also could be
translated, "still ringing in our ears."

Have you ever stood next to an alarm that
unexpectedly went off? It was still ringing in your
ears afterward. John was saying, "I can still hear
the tone of His voice, the inflections that He used.
I hear it still."

When John wrote, "we have seen with our eyes," the words he used in the original language speak of "gazing on something as a spectacle." Have you ever had someone stare at you—and keep staring? I am sure Jesus experienced this on a regular basis. He would probably look down for a moment, look up, and find everyone staring at Him. Also, the phrase, "our hands have handled," could be translated, "with a view to investigate." They scrutinized Jesus' every move.

So the apostles, and certainly John, understood this wasn't just a good man, this wasn't even a great prophet, as much as this was God in human form. John was saying, "We were there. We saw Him. We heard Him. But our fellowship is with the Father, and you can enter into this fellowship with God as well." In fact, there is a special blessing promised to those who have not seen Him but have chosen to believe. After Thomas had seen the risen Lord, Jesus said to him, "Thomas, because you have seen Me, you have believed. Blessed are those who have not seen and yet have believed" (John 20:29). This applies to believers today. Although we have not seen Jesus with our eyes, yet we believe.

WHY JESUS IS UNIQUE

The reason Jesus is so unique above all others is that He was the man who was God. He wasn't a man *becoming* a god. That is impossible. Nor was He one of many gods. He was God who became a man. It will never happen again. This is important, because sometimes we can view God as distant and unapproachable. It reminds me of a story I heard about a little boy who was frightened one night during a great thunderstorm. He called out to his father from his bedroom and said, "Daddy, I'm scared. Come in here."

His Dad, who had settled in for the night and wanted to go to sleep, told the little boy, "Son, it's all right. God is with you in that room right now. You are okay."

There was a moment of silence. Then the little boy shot back, "Dad, right now I need someone with skin on."

That is exactly who Jesus was. He was God with skin on. So if you have wondered what God is like, then take a look at Jesus. If you want to know how God feels toward little children, then look at how children flocked to Jesus. He took them into His arms and blessed them and said, "Of such is the

kingdom of heaven." How does God see a sinner
who is repentant and wants to be forgiven? Look
at how Jesus responded to the woman who had
been caught in the act of adultery. Look at how He
interacted with Zacchaeus and the woman at the
well. You will see that He welcomes sinners with
open arms. Do you want to know how Jesus feels
about hypocrisy? Look at His attitude toward the
Pharisees, for whom He saved His most scathing
words.

The deity of Jesus Christ is
one of the primary themes of this
very Gospel.

The Bible is clear in pointing out that Jesus
Christ was and is God himself. And what sets
John's Gospel apart from the others is that he
doesn't start with the birth of John the Baptist
or even the birth of Jesus. He goes back to the
time before there was a little town called
Bethlehem, and even before there was a garden
called Eden. He even goes back before the time
there was a planet called Earth. John 1:1 tells

us, "In the beginning was the Word, and the Word was with God, and the Word was God." John is pointing out the fact that, even before the creation of the universe, Jesus was always there. John is not suggesting that Jesus had a beginning, because Jesus, being God, is eternal. He has no beginning. He has no end.

The prophet Micah, speaking of Christ's birth in Bethlehem, said, "But you, Bethlehem Ephrathah, though you are little among the thousands of Judah, yet out of you shall come forth to Me the One to be Ruler in Israel, whose goings forth are from of old, from everlasting" (Micah 5:2). "From everlasting" literally means, "from the vanishing point." There is no beginning or end to Jesus Christ, because He is God. There was never a time in which Jesus did not exist, because the word, "was," appears in the Greek imperfect tense, which means, "was continuing." Another way to translate verse 1 is, "In the beginning was the continuing Word and the Word was continuing with God and the Word was continually with God." Our Lord said of himself in Revelation 22:13, "I am the Alpha and the Omega, the Beginning and the End, the First and the Last."

THE GOD-MAN

So don't let anyone ever tell you that Jesus was not God. The deity of Jesus Christ is one of the primary themes of this very Gospel. Yet most cult groups deny the divinity of Jesus.

For example, Jehovah's Witnesses do not believe Jesus was God. Buddhists believe Jesus Christ was a good teacher, but less important than Buddha. Hindus believe that Jesus was just one of many incarnations, or sons of God. They teach that "Christ was not the Son of God," and that "He was no more Divine than any other man and He did not die for man's sins." Muslims believe Jesus Christ was only a man, a prophet equal to Adam, Noah, or Abraham, all of whom are believed to be below Muhammad in importance.

But the Bible teaches that Jesus was the "God-Man" who created everything. So if you are not sure what a group is about, then ask them who they think Jesus was. Was He a messenger, a prophet, or one of many "sons of God?" Or, is He the only Son of God who lived a perfect, sinless life?

There is another twist in the original language regarding the phrase, "the Word was with God." This could be translated, "the Word was continually toward God. God the Father and God the Son were face to face continually." The preposition, "with," bears the idea of nearness, along with the sense of movement toward God. That is to say, there has always existed the deepest equality and intimacy in the Trinity. It is hard for us to grasp the Trinity, the fact that God is a triune being. How can He be Father, Son, and Holy Spirit, and yet be one?

It is a question that many of us have struggled with, sometimes passionately, like the couple I heard about on the news who went to see *The Passion of the Christ*. Somehow, they got into a heated argument afterward about the Trinity. The argument escalated, and by the time they reached their home, it had turned violent. The police had to be called. Upon their arrival, the police arrested both husband and wife. The woman had suffered injuries on her arms and her face, while her husband had a scissors stab wound in his hand. His shirt also had been ripped off. The sheriff, commenting on the incident, said, "It is kind of a pitiful thing to go to a movie like that and fight about it. I think they kind of missed the point."

So let's put our scissors down when we discuss the Trinity. It is hard for us to understand a triune being: Father, Son, and Holy Spirit. But this triune being, this Almighty God, created the heavens and Earth. Many times, we read in the Bible that Jesus was the Creator. According to Colossians 1:16, "For by Him all things were created that are in heaven and that are on earth, visible and invisible, whether thrones or dominions or principalities or powers. All things were created through Him and for Him." He is the hands-on Creator, bringing about all of the things that we see, bringing about our galaxies and our solar system. Hebrews 1:2 tells us that God "has in these last days spoken to us by His Son, whom He has appointed heir of all things, through whom also He made the worlds." There are a lot of worlds, a lot of galaxies, which He made. Scientists tell us there are about one hundred billion stars in the average galaxy, and there are one hundred million galaxies in known space. Einstein believed that with our telescopes, we have scanned only one billionth of theoretical space. This means there is something like ten octillion stars in space. How many is ten octillion? A thousand thousands is one million. A thousand millions is one billion. A thousand billions is a trillion. A thousand trillions is a quadrillion. A thousand quadrillions is a quintillion. A thousand quintillions is a sextillion.

A thousand sextillions is a septillion. A thousand septillions is an octillion. Ten octillions is the number ten with twenty-seven zeros behind it.[1]

"WHY WOULD GOD NOTICE ME?"

He made it all. Jesus Christ created all things. And guess what? This Almighty Creator is interested in you as an individual. Sometimes when we are going through a problem in life, we say, "I don't know what to do. I have exhausted all of my resources. I have tried everything. All I can do now is … gulp … pray!" What an insult to the Almighty God, who brought all of the galaxies and the solar system into existence. We think this is somehow too hard for Him. We think we have a problem He can't unravel.

God wanted to—and wants to—communicate with us.

We think we have a question that He can't answer. We think we have an issue that He can't resolve. But Jesus said, "With God all things are possible" (Mark 10:27).

Just knowing that God is powerful enough to

accomplish what we think is impossible is wonderful. But to realize that this all-powerful, all-knowing God loves us is far more wonderful. Remember, Jesus said, "It is your Father's good pleasure to give to you the kingdom." Then we are told in the Book of Romans, "He who did not spare His own Son, but delivered Him up for us all, how shall He not with Him also freely give us all things?" (8:32). When we have a problem that we bring before the Almighty God, Jesus Christ, the Creator of the universe, He knows what to do.

I read the story of a friend of Henry Ford's named Charles Steinmetz. Apparently, Steinmetz was a mechanical genius. It was said that he could build a car in his mind and also fix it in his mind. One day, the assembly line at the Ford plant broke down, and none of Ford's men could fix it. So they called Charlie Steinmetz. He tinkered for awhile, threw the switch, and it started running again. A few days later, he sent a bill to the Ford Motor Company for $10,000. That is a lot of money today, but back then, it was really a lot of money. The people at Ford were a little surprised. So Henry Ford sent back a letter that said, "Charlie, don't you think $10,000 is a lot for doing a little bit of tinkering?" A little while later, a revised bill from Steinmetz arrived in the mail. This one read, "Tinkering: $10.00. Knowing where to tinker: $9,990."

In the same way, when things go wrong in our lives, Jesus knows where to tinker. He knows how to fix the problem. He knows what to do. He is your Creator. He is your Maintainer. You can trust Him with everything.

Another way you can translate John 1:1 is, "In the beginning was the Communication. ..." "Word" in verse 1 is translated from the Greek word, *logos*.

What this is saying is that the almighty, all-powerful God who created all things became the Word. The Word became flesh. The Word dwelled among us.

God wanted to—and wants to—communicate with us. Ever since humanity's Creation, God has sought to communicate with us in love. We see this from the first book of the Bible to the last. In Genesis, we see the Father looking for Adam in the Garden and asking, "Where are you?" In Revelation, we see God issuing an invitation: "I will give of the fountain of the water of life freely to him who thirsts" (21:6).

God is longing for fellowship with humanity. Why is that? Some would say it is because God is lonely. But God isn't lonely. God doesn't need fellowship with you or me. Rather, He longs for it. He desires it. The Word dwelled among us. The Communication came and walked among us.

GOD IN OUR MIDST

God became a man. Jesus Christ, who has neither beginning nor end, who has always existed, came to this earth as a living, breathing human being. He walked this earth being fully God and fully man. As John 1:5 says, "And the light shines in the darkness, and the darkness did not comprehend it." It was the union of the Infinite with the finite. He who was larger than life became an embryo. Jesus went from the throne of heaven to a feeding trough. He went from the presence of angels to a cave filled with animals. He who sustains the world with a word chose to be dependent upon the nourishment of a young girl.

It is hard for us to imagine both deity and humanity in one person. And while it is true that

Jesus didn't have a sin nature, at the same time, He was exposed to the pressure and the presence of temptation. He experienced thirst, hunger, loneliness, and all of the other emotions that we go through as men and women. A good example of this is the story of Jesus crossing the Sea of Galilee. The Lord was tired from the day's work and fell asleep. Then a radical storm hit and the disciples woke Jesus, saying, "Master, Master, we are perishing!" (Luke 8:24). What could be more human than falling asleep in the boat? But then the Bible tells us, "He arose and rebuked the wind and the raging of the water. And they ceased, and there was a calm" (v. 24). What could be more divine than calming a storm? His own disciples were blown away, figuratively speaking, by this incredible display of power on the part of Jesus. They said, "Who can this be? For He commands even the winds and water, and they obey Him!" (v. 25).

At the cross, we see the same. Nothing could be more human than His crucifixion and death. But nothing could be more divine than the sky darkening and the veil in the temple ripping from top to bottom (not from bottom to top) and Jesus rising from the dead. God, who became a Man, shined

His light on humanity. John tells us, "In Him was life, and the life was the light of men." (John 1:4). This shows God's desire to shed His light, righteousness, and goodness into the world, and indeed, into every crevice of our lives. But sadly, the majority of humanity has rejected this light.

A LIGHT IN THE DARK

It is hard for us to accept that we live in a world of darkness. We like to believe that we are enlightened. As a human race, we are proud of our achievements and our social, technological, and scientific progress. We may point to our advances in computers, communication technology, space travel, and medical science, yet with all of our progress, how far have we really come? We have made no progress whatsoever in changing the basic ills of the human condition. In 1948, General Omar Bradley observed, "We are technological giants and moral midgets." He went on to say, "We have discovered the mystery of the atom, but we have forgotten the Sermon on the Mount." Well said. And how true. But if it was true in 1948, how much more true is it today, and how much more true will it be in the years ahead?

Yes, we live in darkness, a kind of darkness that permeates every level of our society and culture. People cringe when terms such as good, evil, right, and wrong are used. In our day of moral relativism, such verbiage is looked upon as outdated, out-of-touch, and passé. Yet we see a breakdown in the morals of our nation in the abduction of innocent children, senseless violence, and sexual perversion. It seems that everywhere we look, we see more and more darkness. And we realize the heart of humanity has not changed.

Yet the Bible tells us that to know God, we must turn from darkness to light (see Acts 26:18). In fact, the first thing God did in creation was to separate the light from the darkness: "Then God said, 'Let there be light'; and there was light. And God saw the light, that it was good; and God divided the light from the darkness" (Gen. 1:3–4). We make a big mistake when we try to blend what God wants separated.

Those who live in darkness just don't get it when it comes to us Christians. It mystifies them as to how someone can be so committed to their faith. But as John 1:5 tells us, "The light shines in the darkness, and the darkness did not comprehend it."

The word, "comprehend," in the original language carries the meaning of "understood" or "overcome." You don't want to be perceived by unbelievers as a fanatic. You try to relate to them. But they plainly see there is something different about you—something major. The apostle Paul recognized this when he wrote to the Corinthians:

> *Don't team up with those who are unbelievers. How can goodness be a partner with wickedness? How can light live with darkness? What harmony can there be between Christ and the Devil? How can a believer be a partner with an unbeliever? (2 Cor. 6:14–15 NLT).*

Try as you may, and relate as hard as you can, but unbelievers simply are not going to understand our faith and commitment to Christ until their spiritual eyes are opened. According to 1 Corinthians 2:14: "But the natural man does not receive the things of the Spirit of God, for they are foolishness to him; nor can he know them, because they are spiritually discerned." I know this is frustrating to many believers who, more than anything else, want their friends and family to come to know this Jesus who has done so much for them.

We need to just keep shining the light, as Matthew 5:16 tells to do: "Let your light so shine before men, that they may see your good works and glorify your Father in heaven." When you are in a dark place, you don't always appreciate the light coming on. When you're sound asleep in the in the early hours of the morning, when it is still dark outside, you usually don't like it when someone flips on the light and announces that it is time to wake up. But realize that it is this very process of being uncomfortable around true Christians that will help to spiritually awaken an unbeliever.

We are born with an innate sense that there is more to life than what we know.

Before unbelievers can see their desperate need for the light, they must first see that they are living in a miserable darkness. Before there can be conversion, there must be conviction—and that will come through you as you live a godly life and tell them the truth of the gospel. So don't try to undo the very thing God is using in the lives of unbelievers to show them their need for Him.

MORE TO IT THAN THIS

This brings us to an interesting verse that some have misunderstood: "That was the true Light which gives light to every man coming into the world" (John 1:9).

This is not speaking of a light in man, but of God's light shining on man. The Bible tells us that God has set eternity in the human heart (see Eccl. 3:11). This means that we are born with an innate sense that there is more to life than what we know. God designed every man and every woman with a homing instinct, if you will, for something more. That is why, from the moment we were born, we have been on a type of quest—a recognition that there is more to life than we are experiencing.

Sometimes we think, "It is right around the corner ... that next relationship ... that next job ... that next possession ... that next experience. Once I have that, I know I will be happy." But none of this leads to fulfillment, because this homing instinct is driving us toward God—if we will pay attention.

First of all, the evidence of God is everywhere. We read in Romans 1 that the creation around us speaks of God's power and glory. And Psalm 19:1 reminds us, "The heavens declare the glory of God; and the firmament shows His handiwork. Day unto day utters speech, and night unto night reveals knowledge. There is no speech nor language where their voice is not heard" (vv. 1–3). We have this "testimony" of nature that God's light is shining.

Second, God has given each of us a conscience. The apostle Paul spoke of our consciences either accusing or excusing us:

> *(For when Gentiles, who do not have the law, by nature do the things in the law, these, although not having the law, are a law to themselves, who show the work of the law written in their hearts, their conscience also bearing witness, and between themselves their thoughts accusing or else excusing them) in the day when God will judge the secrets of men by Jesus Christ, according to my gospel. (Rom. 2:14–16)*

But what about the people who have never heard the gospel? Will God condemn them to hell? I believe that if someone is a true seeker, then they will become a Christian. Or let me put it another way: If someone doesn't become a Christian, then I do not think he or she is a true seeker. God says in Jeremiah 29, "And you will seek Me and find Me, when you search for Me with all your heart. I will be found by you, says the Lord … " (vv. 13–14).

Yet there are some who believe they don't need to ask God for forgiveness in their lives, because they are relatively moral individuals. "I'm not a sinner!" they may say. But I would invite them to come and stand next to Jesus Christ and see how they compare. How do their lives and actions compare with His? His light shines on us, and that light exposes all of our spiritual and moral deficiencies. But His light is not only there to reveal our shortcomings. It is also there to light the way to our salvation. His light is there so that we can see we are in darkness and can come into His light.

HOW NOT TO BECOME A CHRISTIAN

So how do you come into His light? How do you become a Christian? First, let's look at three ways you cannot become a child of God, according to

John 1:

> *But as many as received Him, to them He*
> *gave the right to become children of God,*
> *to those who believe in His name: who were*
> *born, not of blood, nor of the will of the*
> *flesh, nor of the will of man, but of God.*
> *(vv. 12–13)*

*You cannot be a Christian simply by being
born into a Christian family.* I am amazed at
how some people, when asked how they know they
are Christians, will answer, "Because I think my
grandfather was," or, "Because my mother is a
Christian." It as though they believe their family
has Christian genes. When verse 13 says, "Who
were born, not of blood," it means that Christianity
is not passed on, even if you have Christian parents.
If you do, that is a great privilege. But there has
to come a moment in which you believe. You are
not spiritually transformed because you were
born into a Christian family.

*You cannot make yourself a Christian by your
own will.* Not only does the new birth have nothing to do with your family background, but it also
has nothing to do with desire. "Nor of the will of
the flesh," means that you can't just say, "From this

moment on, I am a Christian." That doesn't make
you a Christian. There has to be a moment where
you come on God's terms, turn from your sin, and
put your faith in Christ. There is a point where we
have to be willing, but it is still God who converts.
As Romans 9:16 says, "So then it is not of him who
wills, nor of him who runs, but of God who shows
mercy." I cannot convert you. Nor can you convert
yourself.

*You cannot become a Christian by sheer
determination.* "Nor of the will of man" means
that being born into God's family has nothing to
do with determination. No one in the world can
make you a Christian. No minister or priest can
make you a Christian by baptism or a sacrament.
You cannot be reborn through a ceremony, or by
reading a creed, or by standing up or sitting down,
or by going forward, or by kneeling at a bench.
None of these things, in and of themselves, will
make you a Christian.

SO WHAT IS A CHRISTIAN?

Now that we've covered how not to become a
Christian, let's look at how to become one. We find
the answer in verse 12: "But as many as received

Him, to them He gave the right to become children of God, to those who believe in His name." Being a Christian is not merely following a creed, though it would include that. It is not merely believing certain truths, though it is that too. It is receiving Christ into your life as Savior and Lord. There has to be a moment in your heart in which you are awakened to your spiritual need and say, "God, I know I am a sinner. I know that I don't measure up. Your light has shined into the crevices of darkness in my life, and You have exposed my spiritual nakedness. You have shown me my vulnerability and my need. Lord, I recognize that I don't measure up. At the same time, I know that I can't become a Christian in my own strength. So I am coming to You on Your terms. I am turning from my sin. I believe that your Son, Jesus, the Word who created all things, became a man and walked among us. I believe that He died on a cross for my sin. I turn from that sin. I put my faith in You. I choose to follow You."

Have you received Him yet? Someone else cannot receive Him for you. You have to receive Him for yourself. Receiving Jesus Christ is not unlike having a gift offered to you. God is offering you a gift. But you need to accept and open the gift.

If you are giving a gift to a man, don't waste a lot of time on the wrapping. Women may appreciate the extra work put in toward making a present attractive. But to a man, wrapping is merely an obstacle. You are keeping him from what he really wants, which is what is in the box. That is all he cares about.

In contrast, women enjoy—and will often prolong—the unwrapping process. I don't understand it, but my wife Cathe is this way. When someone gives her a gift, she will say, "Thank you so much!" Then she will set the gift aside for awhile.

God has given you a gift, but it is not any good until you open it.

I can't do that. If someone gives me a gift, I want to open it immediately. So I will say to her, "Cathe, are you going to open your gift?"

"I'm going to do it later," she will tell me. "I am going to eat dinner first."

"The gift?" I remind her when dinner is over.

"I am going to have dessert," she will say.

"The gift?" I will ask, halfway through dessert.

"I am going to have my coffee."

"Open the gift!" I will say, unable to stand it any longer. "How can you just sit there in the presence of an unopened gift?"

In the same way, God has given you a gift, but it is not any good until you open it. The gift is just sitting there. You think, "I will get to it later. I know it is there. It gives me a good feeling to know it is there. I just love the fact that it is there." But wait a second. You need to receive it. You need to open this gift. Until you have done so, you have not fully received God's forgiveness.

You can say, "I know Jesus is the Lord. I know that He is the Creator of all things. I know that He died on the cross. I know that He has the answer to all my questions. I know that He can forgive me of my sins. He is there knocking. It gives me a good feeling." Hold on. You need to open the door and ask Him to come in. Reach out and receive the gift.

Your Christian family can't do it for you. You can't do it for yourself just by saying, "I believe

in my own way." You have to say, "Lord, I receive
your gift of eternal life, happily and gladly. I choose
to follow Jesus."

Have you done that yet?

"I haven't done it, but I am so close," you say.

I am glad you are close. But consider this:
Until you believe, you are not really any closer to
becoming a Christian than an avowed atheist. Even
though you may intend to believe, my point is that
until you have acted on it, nothing concerning your
eternal destiny has changed. It is not enough to be
close. You also have to believe. You have to receive.
You have to say yes. Have you done that yet? If not,
why don't you do it right now?

"COME AND SEE"

What do you want?" This was the first question to fall from the lips of Jesus during His earthly ministry, and He asks that question of us today: "What do you want? What are you looking for in life?" Some might say they are looking for happiness or success. Someone else may say they want to be loved or that they want inner security and peace. Still others would say they are in search of fame, stardom, and money.

It seems that a lot of people are looking for their fifteen minutes of fame, evidenced by the rising popularity of reality shows such as *American Idol.*

Millions of Americans faithfully cast their votes for their favorite. I think one of the reasons for the incredible success of this show is that people can, in a way, see themselves there. It carries the promise that an ordinary person, involved in a type of glorified nationwide karaoke contest, could rise to the top and become an overnight success. That is the premise of a lot of the reality shows today. Ordinary people like us can maybe become successful. We can reach our dreams. "That could be me," we think.

Years ago, Andy Warhol said that he believed there would come a time when everyone in America would have fifteen minutes of fame. As you look around, it almost seems as though that is indeed the case. But is this really what we should be pursuing in life—mere fame or success or fortune? Let's consider the words of those who already have them. Coming to the end of his life, billionaire Malcolm Forbes said, "By the time we have made it, we have had it." And a very well-known Hollywood celebrity made this statement of her peers:

Nobody would be a celebrity if they weren't severely damaged. Honestly, I think we are damaged people, and so we are looking for the love we never got. Nobody should look up to us or ever do what we do. We are basically circus freaks. None of us is altruistic or any of that. We are pretty selfish and fear-driven people who need help.

Interesting statement, considering how many people today live and die by what celebrities say and do. So what are you looking for in life? What do you want? It is an important question, because it actually will determine the course your life will take. Jesus asked that question of the men in this story before us. He gave these men what they really needed. But first, He wanted to see if they really wanted it, because God will not help the person who does not want His help. This is why Jesus said to the sick man, "Do you want to be made well?" (John 5:6). We may wonder, "What kind of question is that? Of course he would." But not neccssarily. Not every person who is addicted to some substance wants to be free. Not every person who is living in a sinful lifestyle necessarily wants to be free. Not every person, no matter how miserable his or her life is, wants to change. But when you are ready and willing, Jesus will help you.

Jesus gave the men who approached Him more than they bargained for that day, because He got to the real need in their lives. And He will do the same for you. His words to them were, "Come and see," and He is still saying the same today. Let's read about it:

Again, the next day, John stood with two of his disciples. And looking at Jesus as He walked,

he said, "Behold the Lamb of God!" The two
disciples heard him speak, and they followed
Jesus. Then Jesus turned, and seeing them
following, said to them, "What do you seek?"

They said to Him, "Rabbi" (which is to say,
when translated, Teacher), "where are You
staying?"

He said to them, "Come and see." They
came and saw where He was staying, and
remained with Him that day (now it was about
the tenth hour). One of the two who heard
John speak, and followed Him, was Andrew,
Simon Peter's brother. He first found his own
brother Simon, and said to him, "We have
found the Messiah" (which is translated,
the Christ). And he brought him to Jesus.
(John 1:25–42)

Here before us is a classic example of how
various people come to faith in Jesus Christ, as well
as an illustration of how differently Jesus dealt with
each of these people. The first two men, John and
Andrew, heard John the Baptist proclaim Jesus as the
"Lamb of God," and as a result, sought out Jesus for
themselves. Then Andrew, who had begun to follow

Jesus the day before, brought his brother Simon
Peter to Jesus.

———◈◈◈———

*God does the same for all of us at
conversion, which means that we all
essentially have the same testimony.*

———◈◈◈———

Next, there was Philip, who apparently did
not have any believer to really help him, but Jesus
himself sought this person out: "The following day
Jesus wanted to go to Galilee, and He found Philip
and said to him, 'Follow Me.' Now Philip was from
Bethsaida, the city of Andrew and Peter (vv. 43–44).

Last, the newly converted Philip sought out
Nathanael and invited him to come and see
for himself:

> *Philip found Nathanael and said to him, "We
> have found Him of whom Moses in the law, and
> also the prophets, wrote—Jesus of Nazareth,
> the son of Joseph."*
>
> *And Nathanael said to him, "Can anything
> good come out of Nazareth?"*
>
> *Philip said to him, "Come and see."*
> *(vv. 45–46)*

Everyone is different. Perhaps you have heard the testimonies of people who came from radical backgrounds. Maybe they were even involved in gangs, prostitution, or spent time in prison. Then, after coming to faith in Christ, their lifestyle changed dramatically—almost overnight. After hearing testimonies like these, you start to feel as though your conversion may not be as significant as theirs. You think, "Nothing quite that dramatic has ever happened to me!"

But this doesn't mean these believers have a better testimony than you do. It is just a different one.

We need to keep one simple thing in mind: God does the same for all of us at conversion, which means that we all essentially have the same testimony. We all were separated from Him by sin. We all were going to hell. We all came to Him through the cross. So you see, every one of us has a testimony that is worth sharing.

Just as people have different kinds of personalities and temperaments, people come to faith in different ways. Some may have a tremendous emotional experience at conversion, while others may not. I didn't. When I prayed and asked the Lord to come into my life, I didn't feel a thing.

So I wrongly concluded that perhaps I wasn't even converted. But God wants us to live not by feeling, but by faith. As Romans 1:17 reminds us, "The just shall live by faith." However, emotions are not necessarily bad. You may experience God in a very real and profound way. But this does not happen with everyone.

As the passages we have just read illustrate, we all come to Christ differently. Andrew and John found Jesus through a preacher's message. Simon Peter and Nathanael came to Jesus as the result of the personal efforts of a believer. In the case of Philip, there was no human instrument used by God. Which, by the way, is the exception rather than the rule.

GETTING TO KNOW ANDREW

Now I want to look at these individuals one by one. First, there is Andrew. We don't know as much about Andrew as we do about many of the other apostles. He seemed to be an inquisitive person, someone who wanted to know something for himself. John the Baptist, whom Andrew was following, pointed him to Christ.

Understand that at this point, John the Baptist was the greatest prophet of all time. Jesus said, "Among those born of women there is not a greater prophet than John the Baptist" (Luke 7:28). He was the last of a long line of great prophets God had raised up to speak to Israel. He was a major figure and was followed and respected by many. It is worth noting that the ancient Jewish historian, Josephus, wrote more about John than he did about Jesus Christ himself.

So, it was a major event when one day John pointed to Jesus and said, "Look! There is the Lamb of God" (John 1:35 NLT). Any Jew would have readily understood the significance of that statement, because they knew a lamb was used in the sacrificial system to make atonement for the sins of the people. They would understand that John was saying, "There is the one who will take away our sins. There is the Messiah that we have been longing for. That is the One. Follow Him."

You would think that statement alone would be enough to convince a person. So great was John's position as a prophet and spokesman for God that if John the Baptist said to follow Jesus, then that was all one needed to know. Andrew had such great respect for John that he began to follow Jesus, but he wanted to know more about this new leader.

After John the Baptist made his profound statement, Jesus turned around to find John and Andrew following Him. So He asked them, "What do you seek?"

Ever have one of those moments when you were asked a question by a person you have tremendous respect for, and you are not quite sure how to answer? John and Andrew probably were feeling awkward at this moment, unsure of what to say. So they asked Jesus where He lived.

Jesus responded, "Come and see." They were probably thinking that Jesus would take them to a palatial estate somewhere, complete with servants waiting on Him hand and foot. But Jesus perhaps took them to some little place He liked to hang out. Jesus didn't really have a home to speak of, as one of the most telling passages of the New Testament reveals: "And everyone went to his own house. But Jesus went to the Mount of Olives" (John 7:53–8:1). While everyone went to the comfort and safety of a home, Jesus lived in the open air. He himself said,

"Foxes have holes and birds of the air have nests, but the Son of Man has nowhere to lay His head" (Matt. 8:20; Luke 9:58).

John and Andrew stayed with Jesus most of the day. They were discovering that this was indeed the Lamb of God. This was the Messiah. Caution and inquisitiveness were now turning to conviction and belief. Now they knew He was the One they were looking for. This was the very Messiah of Israel, standing before them in flesh and blood.

When it comes to the question of belief, certain people just need to see for themselves. I am the kind of person who will basically come to my own conclusions. I don't like it when people pressure me. If someone wants to sell me something, the worst thing they can do is try to put the pressure on so they can close the deal. If I decide I want to buy something, like a camera for example, I will do all kinds of research. I will read everything there is to read about that particular camera, and then I will check around and find the best deal possible. Then I will go out and purchase it. In most cases, I will know more about the item I am buying than the person who is selling it.

Some people need a little time to investigate things for themselves. After all, if someone can be pressured into a decision for Christ, he or she can be pressured out. If they can be pushed in, they can be pulled out. We need to remember that conversion is the work of God.

What I like about Andrew is that he was always bringing people to Jesus. In John 6, we read of

---

I find it interesting that only one day after he met Jesus, Andrew brought his brother to Him.

Andrew bringing to Jesus a little boy with loaves and fishes in the midst of a hungry crowd. In John 12, we read of some Greek men who were looking for Christ, and Andrew brought them to Jesus. That was his *modus operandi*. He was always doing this. Here, we see him bringing his brother, Simon Peter, to Jesus.

This was a tricky situation, because Peter was the kind of guy who was a little bit larger than life. He was a natural leader, evidenced by his influence on the other disciples. Basically whatever Peter did, the others would do too.

Andrew could have thought to himself, "I am tired of living in Peter's shadow. It is always 'Peter this' and 'Peter that.' If I bring him to Jesus, he will probably try to take this whole thing over. I would like to get a little attention for once. I found the Messiah now. I want to keep it to myself. I don't want Peter to foul it all up."

But Andrew didn't do that. He immediately went out and sought to win his brother to the Lord. I find it significant that only one day after he met Jesus, Andrew brought his brother to Him. That is often the case with new believers. Many times, those who are new in the faith are the most zealous evangelists, while those who have known the Lord for years have grown complacent in their evangelistic endeavors. That should not be the case. In fact, it should be the very opposite.

A MODERN-DAY ANDREW

What it comes down to is this: most people are brought to Christ by someone else. I need to look no further than the staff of Harvest Christian Fellowship, the church where I pastor, to find a great example of this, a modern-day version of Andrew bringing Peter to Jesus.

Mike had been walking with the Lord for about three years when he felt that it was time for him to be more open about his relationship with Jesus. He was working at a bottled water company at the time and realized there were opportunities around him to share his faith. He just needed the boldness to do so.

Jeff, who worked at the same company as Mike, had believed in God for most of his life, but he wasn't a Christian. He tended to judge Christians based on their behavior, and although he saw a lot of hypocrisy, he also saw a lot of authenticity. However, he used the hypocrisy as an excuse for not becoming a Christian. Even then, the authenticity he saw in Mike intrigued him.

Jeff knew Mike was a committed Christian, not so much by the things Mike said, but by how Mike lived. He could see that Mike was very sincere. He was humble, kind, gentle, and stood out from the other guys at work. Mike had recently taken over Jeff's route at the company, and so one day, Jeff found himself riding along in the truck with Mike.

Jeff had already decided ahead of time that if Mike attempted to talk to him about Christianity, he would tell him that in no uncertain terms did he want to discuss it.

"He was about three feet from me all day long," Mike recalls. "It was later in the day that he finally asked me what it was that I was doing. Was I going to church somewhere?"

"As it turned out," Jeff says, "It was the Holy Spirit who opened my mouth—maybe like Balaam's donkey—and I was the one who spoke to Mike."

Mike answered Jeff's questions and shared the gospel with him that day. And when they got back to the office, Mike noticed that Jeff was unusually quiet. He knew something was going on.

"I was really under heavy conviction for the next several days," Jeff says. "God was after me. One night, I just couldn't run anymore. I went into my bedroom, got on my knees, and invited Jesus Christ to be my Lord and Savior. The next day at work, I told Mike about my decision. I am not sure he believed me at first. It took a little convincing, but then he saw that it was genuine."

The following Sunday, Jeff attended Harvest Christian Fellowship for the first time with Mike. Now, more than twenty years later, Mike and Jeff are both pastors at Harvest Christian Fellowship and are serving God faithfully and being used of Him to bring others to Jesus.

A story like this one reminds us that there wouldn't be any Simon Peters if there weren't any Andrews. We celebrate the Simon Peters of the world, but we often forget the Andrews. But for the work of the Kingdom to be done, we need those who are willing to happily and faithfully work behind the scenes. There is no end to what can be accomplished if we are willing to just get the job done instead of worrying about the accolades of others.

Throughout his ministry, Andrew was primarily known as Peter's brother. He was never used of God as publicly as his brother was. Although he was part of the inner circle of disciples, he always seemed to stand in the shadow of Peter, James, and John.

On the other hand, we do not have a record of his bumbling and boasting like we have of Peter's. Nor do we read of his blind ambition as we do of James and John. Andrew serves as the model for all Christians who labor quietly where God has called them. We may not know their names very well, but they are known and greatly loved by the Lord. Andrew is the patron saint, so to speak, of all relatively unknown but faithful followers of Jesus.

ENTER THE ROCK

In contrast to Andrew, we have Peter. I think Peter was the kind of guy who probably dominated any room he walked into. When he encountered Jesus, we see the Lord dealing with him in a completely different way than He had with John and Andrew: "Now when Jesus looked at him, He said, 'You are Simon the son of Jonah. You shall be called Cephas' (which is translated, A Stone)" (John 1:42).

Jesus saw Peter for what he could become. And in time, he indeed grew into his name.

The phrase, "looked at him," also could be translated, "saw right through him." It is the same word that was used to describe the way Jesus looked at Peter after his denial of the Lord

(see Luke 22:61). But it also was a look of love.
There was nothing about Peter that took Jesus by
surprise. He knew exactly what He was getting into
with this big-hearted fisherman. Jesus knew that
Peter was probably full of doubt and uncertainty. So
He wanted to give Peter some hope. Simon means,
"listener," or "hearer," so Jesus said, "You have a new
name. From now on, your name will be The Rock."
The other disciples might have snickered when they
heard this. Yes, Peter was dominant, charismatic,
and outspoken. But he was also unstable, impetuous,
and hotheaded—the very opposite of what comes
to mind at the mention of a rock-like personality.

Sometimes we think of the disciples as one-
dimensional characters living in stained glass. We
speak their names in hushed tones. We even refer
to them as saints. But any honest look at their
stories in the pages of Scripture would reveal otherwise. These men were not saints in the traditional
sense of the word. They were not scholars. They
were not even religious sages. The fact is they were
quite ordinary. They were hopelessly human and
remarkably unremarkable. Yet they were available
and obedient to the Master's call. Jesus did not call

these men to become His disciples because of their greatness. Rather, their greatness was the result of His call.

Just as a great writer can take an ordinary piece of paper and turn it into something of great value, and just as a great artist can turn a canvas worth a few dollars into a priceless work of art, the Creator of the universe, Almighty God, has written His signature on us. He has made His imprint on our lives. Second Corinthians 4:7 reminds us, "But we have this treasure in jars of clay to show that this all-surpassing power is from God and not from us" (NIV).

Jesus saw Peter for what he could become. And in time, he indeed grew into his name.

FINDING PHILIP

We come now to the exception to the rule that God always reaches people through people. Sometimes He just does it himself: "The following day Jesus wanted to go to Galilee, and He found Philip and said to him, 'Follow Me.' Now Philip was from Bethsaida, the city of Andrew and Peter (vv. 43–44). No one specifically reached out to Philip that we know of. So Jesus himself sought him out.

This parallels my own story. No one ever sat down and personally explained the gospel to me. When I was in high school, there were some very outspoken Christians on our campus whom we called Jesus Freaks. My friends warned me to stay away from them. But one day, I saw a girl—a cute girl. She wasn't the most beautiful girl I had ever seen, but there was something about her that caused her to stand out. She had an inward glow that I could not figure out. One day as I was walking across campus, I saw one of my friends talking to her.

I thought, "Here is my opportunity to introduce myself." So I walked up and waited for a break in the conversation. As I waited, I noticed the stack of books she was holding—a couple of textbooks, a notebook, and then one other book with ribbons and gold-edged pages.

"She is one of the Jesus Freaks," I thought. "What a waste of a perfectly good girl!" Still, I introduced myself. She was very friendly, and I thought it would be nice to get know her a little better. I knew she met with the Christians for Bible studies on the front lawn during lunch.

So just out of curiosity, I went to check it out for myself one day. No one invited me. I went on my own. I sat close enough where I could hear what they were saying, but not close enough to look like I was one of them.

As I eavesdropped on their Bible study, I started looking around and thought, "They all kind of glow like she does. Maybe it is not about her at all. Maybe it is something else." Then I thought, "What if those Christians are right and I am wrong? What if they really do have a relationship with God?"

As I considered these ideas for the first time in my life, the young man leading the Bible study, a youth pastor named Lonnie from Calvary Chapel of Costa Mesa, was quoting the words of Jesus from Matthew 12:30: "He who is not with Me is against Me. ..." Then he gave an invitation for people to come to Christ. I found myself getting up, walking over to the group, and going forward with the others who wanted to accept Christ that day. I prayed, and Christ came into my life.

You can probably guess what happened right after that prayer. The attractive Christian girl who initially caught my eye walked up and hugged me.

I thought, "Conversion is good!" Although she was one of my many Christian friends, she never became my girlfriend. But God had used her to get my attention.

The Lord himself intervened in my life, because no one really reached out to me to speak of, and no one had really shared the gospel with me. That is how God reached Philip. And maybe that is how He reached you as well.

NO-NONSENSE NATHANAEL

After meeting Jesus, Philip in turn, sought to introduce someone else to the Lord: "Philip found Nathanael and said to him, 'We have found Him of whom Moses in the law, and also the prophets, wrote—Jesus of Nazareth, the son of Joseph' " (v. 45).

Every heart has its object. If your heart is not seeking Jesus, then it is seeking something else.

Nathanael was a straightforward kind of guy, but he had a sensitive, open heart. Basically, his response to Philip was, "What? Jesus of where?

Nazareth? Can anything good come out of Nazareth?"

Nazareth was an obscure city at that time, but it was known for its wickedness. It was hard to imagine the Messiah coming from such a place.

Of course, Jesus did not come from Nazareth. He was born in Bethlehem, fulfilling the prophecies of the Old Testament. However, Jesus was raised in Nazareth. His followers were later called the Nazarenes, which was meant as an insult. So we can see why Nathanael would say, "Can anything could come out of Nazareth?"

At this point, Philip could have taken offense at Nathanael's question. He could have argued with him. Instead, he simply told him, "Come and see." Philip's response serves as a reminder of how to share our faith. Sometimes we want to arm ourselves with apologetics so that we can blow away anyone who argues with us. We want to pull out the gospel guns, so to speak. We might win the argument that way, but we also might lose the soul.

While there is a place for knowing what we believe and knowing how to share the gospel effectively, we need to remember that it is not about winning arguments. It is not about clever comebacks.

It is about compassion. It is about caring. It is about reaching someone in a genuine way for Jesus Christ.

When Jesus saw Nathanael, He said,

> *"Behold, an Israelite indeed, in whom is no deceit!"*
>
> *Nathanael said to Him, "How do You know me?"*
>
> *Jesus answered and said to him, "Before Philip called you, when you were under the fig tree, I saw you."*
>
> *Nathanael answered and said to Him, "Rabbi, You are the Son of God! You are the King of Israel!"*
>
> *Jesus answered and said to him, "Because I said to you, 'I saw you under the fig tree,' do you believe? You will see greater things than these." (vv. 47–50)*

It would seem to me from the context that something of significance had happened to Nathanael as he sat in the shade of that tree. Maybe he had some kind of encounter with God. Maybe the Lord spoke to his heart. Maybe he was thinking about the Messiah. Then he sees Jesus, who says, "Here is a true Israelite. I saw you under the fig tree."

WHAT ARE YOU LOOKING FOR?

This brings me to the question we started with: "What do you want? What are you looking for?" The answer to that question really reveals your true spiritual state. Everyone is looking for something or someone. Every heart has its object. If your heart is not seeking Jesus, then it is seeking something else.

One of my favorite stories in the Bible is the story of the Prodigal Son. It is about a young man who left the safety, security, and provision of his father's house to go out into the world to find what he could find. He took his portion of his inheritance and wasted it on prostitutes and wild living. He basically made a wreck of his life. One day he came to his senses and decided to go back home. He returned to his father, who welcomed him with open arms, smothered him with kisses, and then said, "Let's have a party. My son who was dead is alive again. He who was lost is found." They prepared a feast, gave him clean clothes, and placed a ring on his finger.

Among this story's many important lessons is the point that everything the son was looking for was already in his father's house. Judging from his actions, what did the young man want? He wanted nice clothes. He wanted to eat well. He wanted to party. But when he went out into the world, he discovered there was a famine in the land. He was starving. He lived in misery and rags.

So he came home to his father and discovered that everything he wanted was waiting for him.

The same is true for you. Everything you are looking for in life is found in Jesus Christ. You can go out into the world and find out for yourself whether that is true. And you will. Or, you can take God's word for it. He is telling you that it is in a relationship with Him.

If you are not certain that is true, then I want to invite you to come and see. That is my answer to you. Come and see.

THE PERFECT GUEST

3

Grow old along with me! The best is yet to be. ..." So goes the famous line from Robert Browning's classic poem. Long before Browning penned the words of "Rabbi Ben Ezra," Jesus communicated a message to His followers in the form of a miracle that said, "The best is yet to be." The place was a wedding in Galilee:

> *On the third day there was a wedding in*
> *Cana of Galilee, and the mother of Jesus was*
> *there. Now both Jesus and His disciples were*
> *invited to the wedding. And when they ran*
> *out of wine, the mother of Jesus said to Him,*
> *"They have no wine."*
>
> *Jesus said to her, "Woman, what does your*
> *concern have to do with Me? My hour has not*
> *yet come."*
>
> *His mother said to the servants, "Whatever*
> *He says to you, do it." (John 2:1–5)*

These verses provide a biblical look at Jesus'

relationship to His mother. This is significant, because this blessed woman of God is often placed on a pedestal—a pedestal she never would have wanted to stand on.

In Jesus' day a Jewish wedding ceremony was a big deal. It could last up to a week, sort of like a bridal shower, bachelor party, family reunion, and honeymoon all rolled into one. During this festive occasion Jesus was attending, the hosts ran out of wine. So Mary, also in attendance, spoke to her son about it.

In addition to sparing their hosts some embarrassment, Mary perhaps had another motive behind the request she made of Jesus: an opportunity to redeem her tarnished reputation. Through no fault of her own, Mary, a godly and morally pure woman, had lived her life under the shadow of suspicion. After being touched by the Holy Spirit and supernaturally conceiving, Mary lived under the cloud of condemnation. She had been immoral, the gossipers would say. She had become pregnant out of wedlock.

On one occasion when Jesus rebuked the Pharisees for their hypocrisy, He told them,

"You are obeying your real father [the devil] when you act that way" (John 8:41 NLT).

They shot back, "We were not born out of wedlock! Our true Father is God himself" (v. 41 NLT). The implication was clear.

For thirty years, Mary had lived with the humiliation of having her character questioned. In asking Jesus to perform this miracle, perhaps she not only was looking for the supply of wine to be replenished, but for vindication as well.

It is important for us to note Jesus' reaction to Mary, because it has been widely taught that the best way to gain access to Jesus is through His mother Mary. Here we see Mary approaching Jesus with a problem. If she had any influence, then He would respond to her request immediately. But notice that He does not: "Woman, what does your concern have to do with Me? My hour has not yet come" (v. 4).

Notice the verbiage Jesus used here. The Greek word used here for "woman" implies respect, but not necessarily warmth. It would be like addressing a woman as, "Ma'am" or "Lady"—a somewhat curious term for someone to use for his mom. It seemed unnecessarily formal under the circumstances. And that is precisely why Jesus used it. He was essentially distancing himself from Mary to some degree. It was a gentle rebuke. It may seem rather cold on the part of Jesus to address His loving mother this way. But what He said was as much for His mother's good as it was for His Father's good: "Ma'am, this is not the way it will be done, because my hour has not yet come."

"My hour has not yet come. …" What did that mean? It was a phrase Jesus used seven times in the gospel of John. What was this "hour" He was speaking of? It was the hour of His crucifixion, resurrection, and ascension. He was speaking of the hour when all of the sin of the world would be poured upon Him and He would be tortured, humiliated, and crucified on a Roman cross. That was the hour—the hour of the completion of His earthly ministry. Ultimately, in the final hours before His arrest, Jesus prayed, "Father, the hour has come" (John 17:1).

What He was saying to His mother was, "Lady, I understand what you are trying to do. I appreciate it, but the time is not right. It will happen when it is supposed to happen."

Like Mary, sometimes we will come to God and say, "I need You to do this right now. I need You to come through for me in this situation." Maybe we see someone getting away with their sin or we hear someone saying unkind things about us. We pray, "Lord, intervene. Do something about this." Sometimes He will say yes. But sometimes He will say, "My hour has not yet come. This is not the time for this to happen. Be patient. Wait on Me."

Mary's response to Jesus is significant, as these are her last recorded words in Scripture. They send an important message to us today: "Whatever He says to you, do it" (John 2:5). That is what our attitude should be as well.

We also find another very important message in these verses: We do not need to go through Mary to get to Jesus. Rather we need to go through Jesus to get to the Father. There is one Mediator between God and men, and that is Christ Jesus (see 1 Tim. 2:5). On the Day of Pentecost when the disciples were waiting for the outpouring of the Holy Spirit, Mary was among them—not in a prominent position, not leading the meeting.

She was simply one of those who were assembled with the others. So let's keep Mary in the proper perspective.

THE FIRST MIRACLE

Here at this wedding, Jesus was about to perform His first miracle. His presence at this wedding signified His divine stamp of approval upon the entire institution of marriage. After all, God is the One who created marriage in the first place—marriage, I might add, between a man and a woman.

I think Jesus probably enjoyed himself as a guest at this wedding He had been invited to. In fact, Jesus is present at every wedding where He is invited, and every marriage as well. I think one reason so many marriages suffer today is because Jesus was not invited to the wedding or to the marriage.

The fact that this was the first miracle Jesus chose to perform may seem a little surprising to us. After all, He could have restored sight to a blind person, healed the sick, or raised someone from the dead. Instead, He chose to turn water into wine.

*Now there were set there six waterpots of
stone, according to the manner of purifica-
tion of the Jews, containing twenty or thirty
gallons apiece. Jesus said to them, "Fill the
waterpots with water." And they filled them
up to the brim. And He said to them, "Draw
some out now, and take it to the master of the
feast." And they took it. When the master of
the feast had tasted the water that was made
wine, and did not know where it came from
(but the servants who had drawn the water
knew), the master of the feast called the
bridegroom. And he said to him, "Every man
at the beginning sets out the good wine, and
when the guests have well drunk, then the
inferior. You have kept the good wine until
now!" (vv. 6–10)*

Jesus performed a miracle that would bring
happiness and joy to those who were celebrating.
That is not to say it was frivolous in any way.
If anything, Jesus demonstrated the unlimited
power at His immediate disposal. At a moment's
notice, Jesus Christ can meet the needs of humanity.
He can always provide what is lacking in earthly
resources.

This is important to remember when we face
what seems to be an impossible situation. Whether
it is the loss of a job, an unexpected illness, or a

The condition of an enlightened
mind is a surrendered heart.

---

failed relationship, none of these things take
God by surprise. And none of them are beyond
His reach.

DOING OUR PART

So Jesus told the servants, "Fill the waterpots with
water" (v. 7). Here we find two important lessons.

One, God want us to trust Him, even when we
don't understand His ways. Notice Jesus *didn't* say,
"Fill the waterpots with water, and it will turn to
wine." Rather, He gave a simple though somewhat
puzzling command.

Often when we are expecting God to reveal His
will in certain situations, He does the same with us.
We say, "Lord, I need to know your will."

"All right," He says. "Then take this first step
of faith."

"What? But I want to know what will happen after that."

"I don't provide blueprints," the Lord might say. "Just take this first step."

We want to know God's will *before* we decide to submit to it. But God wants us to submit to Him before He reveals His will, because the condition of an enlightened mind is a surrendered heart. We find this principle in Romans 12, where the apostle Paul wrote,

> *I beseech you therefore, brethren, by the mercies of God, that you present your bodies a living sacrifice, holy, acceptable to God, which is your reasonable service. And do not be conformed to this world, but be transformed by the renewing of your mind, that you may prove what is that good and acceptable and perfect will of God. (vv. 1–2)*

This passage offers us a conditional promise: You will know what God's will is. But the conditions are: one, that you present yourself to God; two, that you do not conform to this world; and three, that you renew your mind, resulting in a change of attitudes, beliefs, and behavior.

If you want your mind to be enlightened—that is, to know the will of God—then you must surrender your heart.

Two, there is God's part and there is ours. "Fill the waterpots," Jesus said. He was asking them to step out in faith. With a simple word, Jesus could have spoken the wine into existence. But He told the servants to fill the containers with water.

This brings to mind the miracle of the loaves and fish (see Matt. 14:15–18; Mark 6:35–44; Luke 9:12–16; John 6:5–13). Jesus took the loaves and fish, blessed them, and multiplied them. As the food was distributed, there was more. But the disciples had to take that step of faith and distribute what was there.

Maybe God is asking you to do the same right now. Maybe He is asking you to step out in faith, not knowing what will happen next. Maybe He is asking you to start that conversation with an unbelieving coworker. Maybe He is asking you to take the first step through a new door He has opened. As you do your part, God will do His.

That is what the servants at this wedding did, and others were blessed as a result:

When the master of the feast had tasted the
water that was made wine, and did not know
where it came from (but the servants knew),
the master of the feast called the bridegroom.
And he said to him, "Every man at the begin-
ning sets out the good wine, and when the
guests have well drunk, then the inferior.
You have kept the good wine until now!"
(John 2:9–10)

Not only did this miracle impress the other wedding guests, but it impacted Jesus' own followers as well. John tells us, "This beginning of signs Jesus did in Cana of Galilee, and manifested His glory; and *His disciples believed in Him*" (v. 11, emphasis mine).

"His disciples believed in Him," verse 11 tells us, which brings us to the reasons John's Gospel was written: "But these are written that you may believe that Jesus is the Christ, the Son of God, and that believing you may have life in His name" (20:31).

BELIEVING AND LIVING

First, the Gospel of John was written so that unbelievers might believe: "But these are written that you may believe that Jesus is the Christ, the Son of God. ... "

Second, the Gospel of John was written so that we, as believers, may experience more of His life in us: "And that believing you may have life in His name." In the original language, the word for "believing" speaks of a continual action. John is telling us that the more we believe, the more life we will experience. Thus, John wrote this Gospel under the inspiration of the Holy Spirit not only to convince the skeptic, but also to encourage the believer in the commitment he or she has already made.

Jesus said, "I have come that they may have life, and that they may have it more abundantly" (John 10:10). But what does this mean? Does it mean that every Christian will live a really long life? Not necessarily. But it is guaranteeing that every Christian will live a *full* life—a life that is worth living. The abundant life Jesus spoke of is life at its best, life as it was meant to be lived.

At this wedding in Cana, Jesus was saying, "The best is yet to be." And that is what He continues to say to all those who have put their trust in Him. We know that whatever happens, whatever ailments we have, whatever suffering we go through, ultimately for the Christian, the best is yet to be. We will see the Lord one day. We will spend all eternity with Him.

Indeed, the best is yet to be.

QUESTIONS IN THE
DARK

There are certain things in life that we all know. For instance, we know you don't tug on Superman's cape. You don't spit into the wind. You don't pull the mask off the old Lone Ranger, and you don't. … If you know how to complete that sentence, then you are probably over the age of forty-five. And you probably have heard Jim Croce's song, "You Don't Mess Around with Jim," more than a time or two.

We all know certain things, but sometimes we don't know as much as we think we know. We are about to look at a very familiar passage of Scripture—so familiar, in fact, that I think we often skim over it because we have read the story many times before. To do so, however, would be to miss an essential truth of life. What's more, to miss this truth is to miss everything.

A few paragraphs from now, we will read the account of a conversation between a powerful, wealthy, and influential man named Nicodemus

and a carpenter from Nazareth named Jesus.
Nicodemus was famous, highly esteemed, deeply
religious, and yet incredibly empty inside. After
hearing about the great truths that Jesus taught
and the miracles He performed, Nicodemus
approached Jesus one evening after dark.

At this point, you might be wondering what a
conversation that took place so long ago between
a religious man and a Jewish carpenter has to do
with you? Everything. This is not merely a conversation between two men. It is really a conversation
between God and humanity. And if we were to
nominate someone to represent humanity to God,
we would not find a better representative than
Nicodemus.

Nicodemus was a highly intelligent, cultured,
and moral individual. He was as close to fitting
the description of a "good person" as anyone
could hope for. Yet there was something missing
in Nicodemus' life. Despite the fact that he was a
leader in his country and in his faith, Nicodemus
was dissatisfied. So he came to Jesus, looking for
answers. Jesus revealed to him essential truths
for living, as well as the meaning and purpose of

life. The words Jesus gave him have unlocked the
mystery of life for countless millions throughout
the centuries.

YOU MUST BE BORN AGAIN

As we look at their conversation, we will find three
movements in this story. First, we find Jesus and
Nicodemus *face to face.*

> *There was a man of the Pharisees named*
> *Nicodemus, a ruler of the Jews. This man*
> *came to Jesus by night and said to Him,*
> *"Rabbi, we know that You are a teacher come*
> *from God; for no one can do these signs that*
> *You do unless God is with him."*
> *Jesus answered and said to him, "Most*
> *assuredly, I say to you, unless one is born*
> *again, he cannot see the kingdom of God."*
> *(John 3:1–3)*

Jesus was telling Nicodemus that he must be
born again. But what does that actually mean? The
idea here is one of change, of becoming something
different than what you presently are. It implies a
fresh start, a new beginning.

Certainly we are a culture obsessed with change. We need to look no further than our weekly TV schedules to see that. From shows like *Extreme*

Today when people say they are born again, most have no idea what they are talking about.

Makeover, where people volunteer to have their lives radically transformed through things like cosmetic surgery, a new wardrobe, a new hairstyle, and more, to *Extreme Makeover: Home Edition,* where a family's home is radically remodeled in seven days, and *Trading Spaces,* where a room is made over in two days, programs like these prove the idea of change appeals to us.

We like the idea of a fresh start. And when it comes to being "born again," the numbers of those in the United States claiming to have had this experience are higher than ever. Among an approximate 285 million Americans, almost half (46 percent) claim to be "born again." About one-third of American teenagers claim they are born-again believers. Of those, 60 percent believe "the Bible is totally accurate in all of its teachings," and 56 percent feel that their religious faith is very important in their lives.

Yet slightly more than half of all U.S. teens also believe that Jesus committed sins while He was on Earth. About 60 percent agree that doing enough good works will earn them a place in heaven. About two-thirds say that Satan is just a "symbol of evil," and is not really a living being. Only 6 percent of all teens believe there are moral absolutes, and only 9 percent of self-described, born-again teens believe that moral truth is absolute.[2]

In a survey of Christian teens, Josh McDowell found that a slight majority of professing Christian teens now say the bodily resurrection of Jesus Christ never occurred. Nearly 60 percent of evangelical Christian teenagers now say that all religious faiths teach "equally valid truths."[3]

So what is going on here? I would suggest to you that people do not understand what it means to be born again. The very phrase, "born again," has been pirated and emptied of its meaning. It has been dragged through the gutter and given back to us without its power. Today when people say they are born again, most have no idea what they are talking about.

But here in John 3, Jesus settles that for us. He tells us we must be born again, and He tells us what it means.

EVERYTHING GOING FOR HIM

Let's return to the conversation between Jesus and Nicodemus. Verse 1 tells us that Nicodemus was a Pharisee: "There was a man of the Pharisees named Nicodemus, a ruler of the Jews." We often think of Pharisees in a negative light, and understandably so. Jesus had some harsh words for many of them who majored on the minors and were more concerned with the external than the internal. Our Lord saved His most scathing words for the scribes and the Pharisees, calling them "whitewashed tombs" (see Matt. 23:27). We tend to think of all Pharisees as hypocrites, but that is not necessarily the case.

Actually, it was somewhat commendable to be a Pharisee. This was a select group of men, never numbering more than six thousand. Each had taken a solemn vow before three witnesses that he would devote every moment of his entire life to obeying the Ten Commandments. The Pharisees took the law of God very seriously and sought to apply the Ten Commandments to every area of life.

However, the Pharisees were not satisfied with Scripture alone, which is always a problem. They wanted things spelled out more specifically. So a group of people called scribes arose from within the Pharisees. Their job was to spell out how the Ten Commandments were to be applied to every area of life.

The scribes took their work very seriously, and they compiled a thick book called the Mishnah, which the Jews still have to this day. It devotes twenty-four chapters exclusively to the subject

Although Nicodemus came at night, at least he came.

of not working on the Sabbath. In addition to this, the scribes also wrote a commentary on the Mishnah called the Talmud. These devout Jews would spend their lives pouring over these books. And that is what Nicodemus did with his life.

Not only was he from this order, but he also was one of their primary leaders. He was also identified in verse 1 as a "ruler," and therefore was one of the leaders in this very powerful political and religious body known as the Sanhedrin. This ruling body, of which there were only seventy members, was the chief authority in all of Israel. The Sanhedrin was a type of Supreme Court of their day, with this difference: they would intertwine politics and their faith into one. The members of the Sanhedrin would make religious as well as judicial rulings over the lives of the people. So Nicodemus was a member of the elite who would have spent their time studying the Torah (Old Testament Scripture), the Mishnah, and the Talmud.

To arrive at his position would mean that Nicodemus was a careful student of the Torah, the Mishnah, and the Talmud, and must have studied them for many years. In addition to this, Nicodemus was well-known. Jesus referred to him as "the teacher of Israel" (v. 10), which means that Nicodemus was possibly the most popular and prominent teacher in Israel—a household name, if you will.

Even with all this going for him, even though he was famous, highly educated, and deeply religious, Nicodemus sensed there was still something missing in his life. And that brought him to Jesus. The fact that Scripture mentions more than once that Nicodemus' visit took place at night (see John 7:50; 19:39) is worth noting. Perhaps Nicodemus was afraid to be seen talking with Jesus. Maybe he was afraid of what others might think. Or possibly because of the Lord's busy schedule, Nicodemus chose to visit Him at night, because he wanted a little extra time with the Lord. Although Nicodemus came at night, at least he came. In the end, he turned out to be one of the bravest followers of Jesus.

This serves as a reminder that in everything, there must be a beginning. Some have an outwardly impressive beginning with Jesus, only to deny Him later. Take Judas Iscariot, for example. He was an apostle when Nicodemus was still groping his way along, looking for answers to his questions. But at the end of the Lord's ministry, Judas betrayed Jesus and went and hung himself, while Nicodemus stepped forward. He joined Joseph of Arimathea in preparing the body of Jesus for burial (see John 19:38–40). So even if you may have had a feeble beginning,

you can have a strong finish. That is better than
having a strong beginning and no finish at all.

TIME WAS OF THE ESSENCE

Let's return to the conversation. Imagine how
nervous Nicodemus must have been as he prepared
to see Jesus. In nervous anticipation, he may have
recited his lines over and over again. But in spite of
his position and influence, Nicodemus approached
Jesus with the greatest respect: " 'Rabbi, we know

*There is no such thing as a Christian
who is not born again.*

that You are a teacher come from God; for no one
can do these signs that You do unless God is with
him' " (v. 2). For a man like Nicodemus to call Jesus
"Rabbi" was an amazing thing. It was an important
acknowledgement. Being the teacher in Israel,
Nicodemus was familiar with the prophets and their
words concerning the Messiah. If he had specifically studied Daniel, he would have known that the
Messiah's first coming actually had been predicted
for this time in history. According to Daniel's

prophecy, the Messiah was present somewhere in Israel and would soon be put to death. Nicodemus could not waste any time.

Add to this the fact that Nicodemus may have been getting on in years. He may have been an elderly man when this conversation took place. "How can a man be born when he is old?" he had asked Jesus (v. 4). The statistical cards were stacked against him. This might explain the cautious manner in which he approached Jesus. It reminds us of how hard it can be to reach those who have been steeped in manmade religion for many, many years. Still, Nicodemus was not beyond the reach of Jesus. Neither are you, no matter what age you are.

Nicodemus began his question with the phrase, "We know." Yet he had come to Jesus alone. He wasn't ready to say, "I know." In a sense, he was probably hiding behind this phrase, just as people say, "I have a friend who wants to know. ..." But Jesus immediately got to the point, because He knew exactly what Nicodemus needed. With a single, sharp, and penetrating phrase, Jesus sliced through all the layers of rules and legalistic

attitudes that had accumulated in the mind of
Nicodemus:

> *"Most assuredly, I say to you, unless one is*
> *born again, he cannot see the kingdom of*
> *God." (v. 3)*

"Most assuredly," means, "I tell you the truth."
In other words, Jesus was saying, "I am about
to reveal a fundamental reality of life to you,
Nicodemus. Listen very carefully!" Like a sword,
these words pierced this Pharisee's heart. This is
not optional. This is essential. This is absolute. It is
the life-changing truth that I was speaking of at the
beginning of this chapter: you must be born again.
Jesus was saying, "Nicodemus, your religious beliefs
are not enough. In spite of the fact that you are at
the top of the heap in your religion, it means nothing. It has not brought you any closer to heaven."

"BORN AGAIN" DEFINED

As I have already pointed out, there is a lot of
confusion today regarding what the term, "born
again," means. Here, Jesus is helping us to see what

it really means, which is, "to be born from above."
Some people will say, "I am a Christian, but I am
not one of those 'Born Agains.' " But there is no
such thing as a Christian who is not born again.

But why must we be born again? Why do we
need a spiritual rebirth? We find the answer in
verse 3: " 'Unless one is born again, he cannot
see the kingdom of God.' " This is why unbelievers cannot understand when Christians try to
explain what Jesus Christ has done for them. As
1 Corinthians 2:14 tells us, "But the natural man
does not receive the things of the Spirit of God, for
they are foolishness to him; nor can he know them,
because they are spiritually discerned." Another
translation puts it this way: "But people who aren't
Christians can't understand these truths from
God's Spirit. It all sounds foolish to them because
only those who have the Spirit can understand what
the Spirit means" (NLT).

Jesus said, "Unless one is born again, he cannot
see the kingdom of God" (v. 3). So what exactly did
Jesus mean by "the kingdom of God?" The kingdom
of God has a past, present, and future application.

The past application of the kingdom of God was when Jesus walked this earth. He gave us a glimpse, a sneak preview of what is to come. On one occasion Jesus said, "The Kingdom of God has arrived among you" (Luke 19:20 NLT). He was referring to His presence among the people. He was saying, "I am walking among you. The kingdom of God is here." That was the past application.

The present application of the kingdom of God is when we personally live under the rule and reign of Jesus Christ. The Bible tells us, "For the kingdom of God is not eating and drinking, but righteousness and peace and joy in the Holy Spirit" (Rom. 14:17). The idea is that of Christ ruling and reigning in your life. This is what Jesus was referring to when He said, "But seek first the kingdom of God and His righteousness, and all these things shall be added to you" (Matt. 6:33).

The future application of the kingdom of God will be when Christ comes back to establish His kingdom on Earth. This will be when the lion will lie down with the lamb (see Isa. 11:5–7) and the earth will be filled with the knowledge of the Lord (see Isa. 11:9; Hab. 2:14).

Here is what Jesus was saying to Nicodemus:

- "You will not see the kingdom of God *presently* unless you realize who I am."
- "You will not experience the kingdom of God *internally* until you open your heart to my rule and reign."
- "You will not live in the kingdom of God *externally* until you are born again."

So when we pray, "Your kingdom come, your will be done," we are praying for the rule of Christ in our lives and for the day of His return.

LET'S GET REAL

Next, we find Jesus and Nicodemus *mind to mind* (John 3:4–8). Jesus had the Pharisee's attention. Nicodemus was engaged. So he asked, "How can a man be born when he is old? Can he enter a second time into his mother's womb and be born?" (v. 4).

Can we really become different than who we are?

Nicodemus was essentially saying, "Lord, I accept what you say in premise, but how can I start over again? Is it really possible to be born all over again? I mean, obviously you can't enter into your mother's womb. What are you talking about here?"

This is a good question, because we do wonder whether a person really can change. Can they really become different than what they are? After all, how many times have we tried to change ourselves? We make resolutions to lose weight, exercise more, watch less TV, and read the Bible more often. We try new clothes or maybe a new job. But can we really change?

Years ago, my oldest son Christopher had a little pet rat, ironically named Nicodemus. He was a really cute little rat, and we all grew to like him. He was like a member of the family. But Christopher began to feel sorry for Nicodemus and the fact that he lived in a mere cage. Christopher was convinced that his little rodent friend needed a shelter of some kind, so he decided to build one for him. He constructed a very clever little house out of balsa wood, complete with a little roof, little windows, and a tiny front door that opened and closed. Over the door, Christopher hung a little sign that read, "Nicodemus." I think it gave us all a good feeling when we went to bed that night, knowing Nicodemus had his own little

house to sleep in. The next morning, we got up to
find the house missing and Nicodemus looking a
little plumper. He had eaten his house! Nicodemus
didn't get it. He didn't understand that it was his
house. He simply thought, "This looks good. I think
I will eat it." Why? Because he was a rat, that is why.
We may have attached human attributes to this
little rodent and gave him his own house to sleep
in, but the fact is that a rat is still a rat. We could not
change his nature.

But is it possible to change the nature of a
human being? Can we really become different than
who we are? That is the question Nicodemus was
asking. And that is the question we are still asking
today. Jesus' answer was yes—only when the Spirit
of God does it.

Maybe at this point Jesus and Nicodemus felt
a warm breeze blowing, which prompted an illustration: "The wind blows where it wishes, and you
hear the sound of it, but cannot tell where it comes
from and where it goes. So is everyone who is born
of the Spirit" (v. 8).

In other words, Jesus was asking, "Can you see
the wind, Nicodemus?"

"No."

"But do you see its effect?"

"Yes."

"So is everyone who is born of the Spirit," Jesus was saying. "You can't see this with your eyes, but you can see the work of God that takes place in the human heart."

I read an article about a town that had been hit hard by a storm all night long. In the morning, the residents of the town were amazed to find a common, plastic drinking straw driven deep into a telephone pole by the powerful winds of the night before.

We may not see the wind, but we can see its effect. The same is true when you have been born from above by the Holy Spirit.

THE ABCs OF THE GOSPEL

Last, we find Jesus and Nicodemus *heart to heart* (vv. 9–21). I think there might have been desperation in Nicodemus' voice at this point. "How can these things be?" (v. 9).

"Are you the teacher in Israel and you don't know these things?" Jesus asked. The implication here was that Nicodemus was famous. He was respected. He was well-studied. Yet he didn't understand this. And being a student of Scripture, Nicodemus certainly should have known there were passages in the Old Testament that even alluded to what our Lord was speaking of when He said, "You must be born again." One such verse is Ezekiel 11:19, where God said, "Then I will give them one heart, and I will put a new spirit within them, and take the stony heart out of their flesh, and give them a heart of flesh." This was pointing to the born-again experience. "Nicodemus, it can happen," Jesus was saying. "You should know this from studying the Word."

Apparently, Nicodemus' religion had not prepared him for what he really needed. So Jesus laid out to Nicodemus the ABCs of the gospel: "And as Moses lifted up the serpent in the wilderness, even so must the Son of Man be lifted up, that whoever believes in Him should not perish but have eternal life" (John 3:14–15).

Jesus was sending Nicodemus back to familiar territory: the Scriptures, specifically Numbers 21. Nicodemus would have known this story from Israel's wilderness wanderings. The Israelites were complaining that God had abandoned them. They accused Moses and God of failing them and of bringing them to the wilderness to die. They were sick of what God had provided for them. So the Lord sent venomous snakes to bite them. They quickly came to their senses and sought Moses' help. So God instructed Moses to erect a pole with a serpent of brass wrapped around it. Whoever looked at that serpent on the pole was healed of his or her snakebite.

God did everything He could do. The Israelites simply had to look at that pole. They could have known of the pole's existence, yet chosen not to look. But if they wanted to be healed, then they needed to look at the pole.

That was a picture of what Christ would do on the cross. We all have been bitten by the serpent, Satan. We have his deadly venom in our system.

We must quickly find the antidote, and it is provided through Christ and His shed blood on the cross. If we will look to Jesus for salvation, we will be forgiven. In fact, on the day that Jesus hung on the cross, some looked, and believed (Matt. 27:54; Mark 15:39; Luke 23:42–43, 47). Others looked and turned away (Matt. 27:39–44; Mark 15:29–32; Luke 23:35–39). And that is what it ultimately comes down to. Either you will look and live,

I fear for those who say they believe, but never have repented.

or you will look and leave. As Isaiah 45:21–22 says, "And there is no other God besides Me, a just God and a Savior; there is none besides Me. Look to Me, and be saved, all you ends of the earth! For I am God, and there is no other."

WHAT BELIEVING MEANS

Jesus pointed Nicodemus to this simple truth. Then He brought it all together in the most well-known verse of the New Testament, John 3:16: "For God so loved the world that He gave His only begotten Son, that whoever believes in Him should not perish but have everlasting life." Many picture God as some kind of cosmic killjoy who is out to ruin their lives. But the truth is that God loves you. He wants to have a relationship with you. We can talk about love all day long, but God showed His love for us in a tangible way: "But God demonstrates His own love toward us, in that while we were still sinners, Christ died for us" (Rom. 5:8).

Jesus came to this world not to come down on people, but to reach out to people. While religion tells us what we must to do reach up to heaven, God reached down from heaven by sending His Son, Jesus. We are not reaching out to God, trying to earn His approval. Rather, it is God reaching out to us. That is the message of the gospel. It is a message that Christ, who lived a perfect life, died on the cross in our place, and shed His blood for us, now offers us the gift of eternal life if we will believe.

But what does it mean to believe? So many people say they believe. But *what* do they believe? The Bible says, "Even the demons believe—and tremble!" (James 2:19). To believe does not simply mean intellectually accepting something to be true. To believe means to "adhere to, commit to, have faith in, rely upon, and trust in." It comes back to the issue of being born again. To be born again, to be a believer, means not only embracing Christ and Christ alone for salvation, but also turning from your sin. Repentance is a part of belief, like two sides of a coin.

I fear for those who say they believe, but never have repented. As the statistics cited earlier in this chapter indicate, there is a lot of confusion regarding the definition of the terms "Christian" and "born again." But how can someone claim to be a Christian and not believe that the Bible is the Word of God? How can someone claim to be born again and believe that Jesus sinned, when the Bible says He never sinned? How can someone claim to be a real follower of Jesus and yet reject what the Bible clearly teaches? Answer: they can't.

IS IT CHOOSING? OR BEING CHOSEN?

How about you? Do you know that you have eternal life? Do you have the assurance of salvation? The choice is yours as to what you will do with this wonderful gift of God. You can gladly accept it or reject it. When someone offers you a gift, you either take it or reject it. You cannot say, "I'm neutral on this. I can't decide." Some people may say that they have no choice in the matter, that God does the choosing and not us. They believe that you are

either predestined to heaven or to hell. Those of
the Calvinistic persuasion would lean toward over-
stressing the sovereignty of God, and for all practical purposes, do away with the choice of humanity
in the matter.

Those of the Armenian point of view would
tend to dismiss the sovereignty of God and instead
emphasize the free will of humanity.

Do you know a Nicodemus?
A religious person?
A moral person?

I do not subscribe to either point of view whole-
heartedly. I do believe in the sovereignty of God
and predestination. However, I reject the idea of
irresistible grace and limited atonement, because
I believe the grace of God is resistible, though not
easily. I also believe that Jesus Christ died for all
the world, not just the "elect." Otherwise, why
would the Bible say, "Today, if you will hear His
voice, do not harden your hearts" (Ps. 95:7–8;
Heb. 4:7)? This implies, along with other countless
passages, that the heart can be hardened and grace
can be resisted.

Christ did not die for the elect, but for the world: "For God so loved *the world* that He gave His only begotten Son … " (John 3:16, emphasis mine). And, "While we were *still sinners,* Christ died for us" (Romans 5:8, emphasis mine).

One the other hand, there is free will. We must personally choose whether we will put our trust in Jesus Christ for our salvation. It is an undeniable fact that Jesus said, "You did not choose Me, but I chose you … " (John 15:16).

So how do I reconcile these two approaches? I don't. And thankfully, I don't have to. I simply follow the scriptural emphasis, recognizing that God's sovereignty and man's responsibility are taught side by side in the same Bible.

Jesus will receive and reveal himself to any person who will come to Him honestly and heart to heart, just as He did with Nicodemus. "Everyone who believes in him will not perish but have eternal life" (John 3:16 NLT). So don't give up on the unbeliever you have been praying for. And don't give up on yourself. Jesus said, "The one who comes to Me I will by no means cast out" (John 6:37).

GOOD PEOPLE NEED GOD TOO

Do you know a Nicodemus? A religious person?
A moral person? I would like to tell you about
one that I knew. His name was Oscar Laurie, and
he was an attorney who lived in New Jersey. My
mother, who was married and divorced many times,
married him while I was still a young child, and
he adopted me. Oscar Laurie was the only man
during my childhood who actually treated me as
a father should treat a son. When I messed up, he
would discipline me. When I did well, he would
commend me. He taught me respect, and he taught
me manners. Because he treated me as his son, I
respected him and loved him, which is why it was
hard when I got out of school one day and the car
was loaded up. When I asked my mom where we
were going, she told me we were going to Hawaii.

"Where's Dad?" I asked.

"He's not coming," she told me.

My mother left him and married another
guy, and on it went.

After I became an adult, I really wanted to
see Oscar Laurie again. I wanted to tell him
about what Christ had done for me, because

I had become a Christian at the age of 17. With the help of someone from our church who worked for a bar association, I was able to get in touch with him. He told me that he wanted to see me, and so I mentioned that I would be coming to New York soon for a speaking engagement and suggested that we have lunch.

He said, "No, come stay at our house." Because he had remarried and had a family, I didn't want to impose. But he insisted. So I went to my speaking engagement, and when I got off the train and saw him, I immediately recognized him. He hadn't even changed that much. As we spent a little time together, I found out that he had recently had a heart attack and had almost died. So one night, after his wife had made a wonderful Italian meal, we were sitting around the table and talking. His wife said, "Well, Greg, tell me about how you became a Christian and a pastor."

As I shared my story, his wife was very responsive. My dad, on the other hand, sat at the other end of the table, listening quietly, like an attorney in a court of law. I thought, "This is not going well." But he reminded me a little bit of Nicodemus.

He was a moral man. He was an educated man. He was a good man, a man of integrity. But he didn't have Christ living in him.

At the end of the evening, he said, "Well Greg, do you want to go walking with me in the morning?" (The doctor had advised him to get exercise because of his heart condition.)

I said, "Sure, Dad. What time?"

He said, "I will knock on your door at 6:00." Well, that meant 3:00 a.m. California time, but the knock on the door came the next morning, and I got up, rubbing the sleep out of my eyes. As we started to walk along, he said, "Greg, I listened very carefully to what you said last night, ..." (suddenly I am awake) "and I want to become a Christian right now."

I was shocked—shocked that he said that.

So he said, "I ... I want Jesus to come into my life."

I couldn't believe it. I didn't even think he had been responding to what I was saying the night before. So I said, "Well, Dad, let me go over that one more time." And I went over the whole thing again.

Then he said, "Yes, that is what I want to do."

"Well, we should pray," I told him.

He said, "Let's pray right now." So he got down on his knees. There we were in a park, on our knees. As we prayed, tears flowed down the cheeks of this not-so-emotional man. When we finished, he said to me, "I know the Lord has come in." Then he added, "Let's pray for my heart condition. God can heal me too."

So we prayed. Then, when we were done praying, he said, "I know I am saved. And I think the Lord has healed me. Let's go tell my doctor."

"Now wait, Dad," I said. "Hold on. I don't know if God has healed you."

"Well, I think He has." So we went to his doctor's office. We walked in, and my dad told his Jewish doctor, "I just got saved, and Christ is in my life, and I am healed."

It was hard for me to leave New Jersey and to return home to California, but I located a church for him to attend and told him, "Dad, just start reading the Bible and I will be back."

Three weeks later, I returned. I was afraid he wouldn't be doing well. So I said, "Well, let's read something from the Bible. ..."

I read a verse, and he said, "Oh, right. That is Paul in Ephesians, right?"

"Yes it is. That's right."

As we went on, I discovered that he had read the entire Bible while I had been away. And it started changing his life. He got involved in his church and eventually became an elder. He got involved with The Gideons International and helped distribute Bibles. He served the Lord for the rest of his life. Now he is in heaven, and I am looking forward to seeing him again someday.

Maybe you know people like Oscar Laurie. You know they are not radical sinners. They are not drug users, alcoholics, or party animals. They work hard. They pay their taxes. They are trustworthy. They are dependable. You have told them about Christ, but nothing has happened. You think it is never going to work.

Remember Nicodemus. And remember my dad. While they didn't know Christ, they saw their need and came to faith in Him. So keep praying, and don't give up.

God can change each one of us—if we will come to Him on His terms. We can experience a true "extreme makeover," not on the outside, but on the inside.

5 A DIVINE DETOUR

Charlene McDaniel was a beautiful young woman. Some even compared her to Marilyn Monroe, which was pretty heady stuff for someone from Friendship, Arkansas. Charlene was one of nine children of Charles and Stella McDaniel. Although she had been raised in a Bible-teaching Baptist church, she bristled at the idea of following God's Word and not being free to do what she wanted to. The bright lights of the big city were calling, and she felt the fastest road to the lifestyle she longed for was to marry young.

This marriage would be the first of seven, perhaps eight, to come. During her first marriage, Charlene gave birth to her first of two sons. But feeling her husband was not the man she was looking for, she divorced him.

She married again, and after the anguish of giving birth to a stillborn child, she returned to the party scene, looking for something more exciting than married life. She had a fling with a man whom she met in Long Beach and then found out she was pregnant. Back in the early 1950s, having children out of wedlock was not as common as it is today, so she married again and had her second son. Charlene's extended family nicknamed this son Pogo, because, according to his aunt,

---

> *People would not even look at her; much less give her the time of day.*

"He was always so cute and mischievous, like the little opossum character in the cartoon strip."

Charlene's first son lived with his grandmother while his father was in the military, and her second son, Pogo, was sent to military school for a time and also lived with his grandparents and extended family. Charlene could not keep passing him off, so Pogo lived with his mom as she made her way from one dead-end relationship to another, marrying and divorcing again and again. While Pogo was with his mother, all he saw was partying and violence, and he watched one husband in particular nearly kill her one night.

Charlene was on a quest, a search for happiness. Pogo accompanied her on that quest as she went from man to man and from marriage to marriage. These were frightening times for a young boy. He didn't know where his mother was when she wouldn't come home at night. Or when she returned home at four o'clock in the morning, she would pass out from a hard night of drinking. But he felt that his mother had no one to care for her but him, so he did his best as a ten-year-old boy.

I know that for certain, because I was the mischievous Pogo, and Charlene was my mother.

BACK TO HER ROOTS

As I was exposed to this hedonistic world of my mom's, I thought there must be more to life than this. Yet ironically, by the time I reached my mid-teens, I had begun to follow in my mother's footsteps. Then something unexpected happened in my life. I came to Christ at age seventeen, and I suddenly found myself trying, along with my grand-parents, to call my mother back to her spiritual roots.

My mom bristled at such an idea and completely resisted all my efforts—or so it seemed. I saw little glimmers of hope here and there, but for the most

part, there was no change. She was still on that
search and simply could not imagine she would
find what she had been looking for in the roots of
her spiritual upbringing.

As the years passed by, her once-legendary
beauty began to fade. All the drinking, smoking,
and hard living began to take its toll, and one night,
while driving under the influence, she had an accident that horribly disfigured her face. Her beauty,
the one thing she had counted on throughout her
life, was gone.

I saw my mom begin to soften. She would wait
for a prayer before a meal. She always seemed
proud of me and was glad to tell everyone that I
was her son. And although I didn't know it at the
time, she saved every newspaper clipping about
Harvest Christian Fellowship and about the
Harvest Crusades we have been holding nationally
and internationally since 1990.

After she discovered she had kidney failure and
would need dialysis three times per week, she began
returning to her spiritual roots. One month before
her death, I had a very direct conversation with her. I
asked her if she believed in Jesus Christ as her Savior

and Lord. I then told her that she ought to be coming to church. And the next Sunday, she came.

Her search brought her back to what she knew as a young girl. Like the Prodigal Son, she returned. But sadly, she spent almost all her life looking to men and to romance for fulfillment. Yet all along, that fulfillment could be found in a relationship with Jesus Christ.

AN APPOINTMENT WITH GOD

We are about to look at another story of a woman who was a lot like my mother. Or, perhaps I should say that my mother was a lot like her. We know her as the woman at the well, an empty person who thought that romance and sex would fill the void in her life. She went from husband to husband, hoping to find her prince. But after five husbands, she simply gave up. She was disillusioned, scorned, and ignored. People would not even look at her; much less give her the time of day. That is, until Jesus came along.

As we will see, Jesus had an appointment with her. Of course, she didn't know anything about it, but He did. And Jesus always keeps His appointments.

Until she met Jesus, she did not realize that

an intense spiritual thirst had been driving her.
Not only do we see a searching, spiritually thirsty
person in this story, but we also see the Master
Evangelist himself in action, instructing us by
example in how to share our faith. Our story opens
in John 4:

> He left Judea and departed again to Galilee.
> But He needed to go through Samaria. So
> He came to a city of Samaria which is called
> Sychar, near the plot of ground that Jacob
> gave to his son Joseph. Now Jacob's well was
> there. Jesus therefore, being wearied from
> His journey, sat thus by the well. It was about
> the sixth hour. A woman of Samaria came
> to draw water. Jesus said to her, "Give Me a
> drink." For His disciples had gone away into
> the city to buy food. (vv. 3–8)

A little historical background will help us
understand some important things about this
passage. No Orthodox Jew would ever travel
through Samaria to Galilee. In fact, an Orthodox
Jew would go out of his way to avoid Samaria
altogether. Most Jews of Jesus' time, if they wanted
to travel from Judea to Galilee, would take the

long way around. This would take about five days, even though there was a direct route from Judea to Galilee, which was about seventy miles, or the equivalent of a two-and-a-half-day walk. The reason most Jews chose the longer route over the more direct one was prejudice, pure and simple. The Jews did not want to associate with the Samaritan people, preferring to endure the long, uncomfortable road rather than to let go of their bigotry.

But Jesus chose the shortcut, not because it was easier, but because He had to. Why? Because there was a hurting, lonely, and searching woman in Samaria. In spite of the strong, deeply rooted prejudice between these two groups of people, Jesus had to go.

This shows us that the love of God knows no racial, economic, or sinful boundaries. Long before the creation of the world, it had been settled in eternity that Jesus was to meet a burned-out, immoral Samaritan woman that day. She did not realize it at the time, but she had an appointment with God.

OUT OF THE COMFORT ZONE

As we look at this detour Jesus took, we see a number of truths about being used by God.

First, if we want to be used by God, then we need to reach out to people who are not necessarily just like us. Conventional wisdom may tell us that we should find someone who is of the same age and vocation as us, and then share the gospel,

---

Every generation needs regeneration, and ours is no exception.

---

because we can relate to someone like who is just like us. A trend in churches today is to essentially design a church that will reach a certain demographic. Some churches may try to reach the more affluent, while others might concentrate their outreach primarily to bikers or surfers or intellectuals or a certain racial group. While I applaud all efforts to reach different types of people, I personally want to see a church service in which a biker sits next to a surfer, a person of affluence sits next to a person with a lower income, and in which a

broad spectrum of racial groups is represented. I
want to see a church in which those boundaries
are dropped as believers fellowship together. That,
to me, is the genius and the beauty of the church
itself. As Galatians 3:28 tells us, "There is neither
Jew nor Greek, there is neither slave nor free, there
is neither male nor female; for you are all one in
Christ Jesus."

But John's Gospel indicates that this Samaritan
woman was a social outcast, because she came to
the well at noon, the hottest part of the day. As she
approached the well with her water pot, she saw
this Jewish man sitting there and braced herself for
what she was sure would be another confrontation.

An ordinary Jew would have thrown it to the
ground if a Samaritan had offered him a cup of
water. But Jesus requested one from her. Now,
Jesus was frequently called "Rabbi" by those who
approached Him, and according to Jewish law,
Rabbis were never to talk to a woman in public,
not even to their wives or sisters. Rabbinical law
stated, "It is better to burn the law than to give it
to a woman." This had been taken to such extremes
that when a Pharisee would see a woman in public,
he would cover his eyes, often causing him to bump

into walls or other objects. They were known as "the bruised and bleeding Pharisees." Of course, this was silly legalism and religion at its worst.

So whom did Jesus choose to engage in conversation and share His great truth? A woman—and an immoral one, at that. To add insult to injury, she was a Samaritan woman. In other words, she was the lowest of the low.

So let's learn from Jesus' example and be willing to reach out to those who may not be just like us. God may lead you to share your faith with someone you may not be comfortable with. We need to be open to reach the category of people God invites to believe, which is, "whoever." As John 3:16 tells us, "Whoever believes in Him should not perish but have everlasting life."

LEARN TO LIKE PEOPLE

Second, if we want to be used by God, then we have to go to where people are. I remember visiting a central California farm, where the owner shared some words of wisdom that his father had passed along to him. "For the fruit to grow," his father said, "the farmer's shadow has to fall on the field."

In other words, the farmer needs to be in the field, watching and harvesting his crops. We must do the same.

This is what Jesus was doing. He was going out of His way to where a person was. After all, the Bible does not say that the whole world should go to church. Rather, it says that the church should go to the whole world.

Third, if we want to be used by God, then we need to care about the people we speak to. Verse 4 tells us that Jesus *"needed* to go through Samaria" (emphasis mine). When the apostle Paul was in Athens, his spirit was stirred, or provoked, when he saw the people given over to idolatry (see Acts 17:16).

Any effective sharing of one's faith always will begin with a God-given burden. Paul said, "Woe is me if I do not preach the gospel!" (1 Cor. 9:16). Is your spirit stirred when you see a culture largely given over to sin, when you see men and women (especially young men and women) throwing their lives away as they chase after empty dreams and pursuits? Every generation needs regeneration, and ours is no exception. This brings us to our next principle.

IT PAYS TO PERSEVERE

Fourth, if we want to be used by God, then we need to keep at it, even when we are tired. We read in verse 6: "Jesus therefore, being wearied from His journey, sat thus by the well." Though He was God, He never used His miraculous powers to help himself. His disciples were going away into another city to buy food. Here was Jesus, who was weary in His search for sinners and had become thirsty, seeking those to whom He would soon offer the water of life. Here was the Creator of the universe, who miraculously provided bread and fish for thousands to eat in the wilderness, waiting for His disciples to get some food. Had He chosen to, He could have spoken a pizza and a Coke into existence (before they had been invented). Jesus must have been exhausted, because He stayed back, even though the disciples went into town for food.

Jesus rarely had a moment to himself. His ministry was not only physically draining, but it was emotionally and spiritually draining as well. That is why He spent nights in prayer to recharge.

Often, we guard against burning ourselves out in busyness. And that is okay. I have heard some say

they are "burned out" in their ministries and they
can't go on. But in more than thirty years of having
the privilege of serving the Lord, I can honestly say
I have never been tired *of* service. But I have been
tired *in* it. What better thing to be tired from than
a life spent in service to God? That is never a waste.

Jesus told a story about a foolish man who failed
to take into consideration things of eternal value.
This man said, "I will do this: I will pull down my
barns and build greater, and there I will store all
my crops and my goods. And I will say to my soul,
'Soul, you have many goods laid up for many years;
take your ease; eat, drink, and be merry'" (Luke
12:18–19). That is exactly what people say today:
"Take it easy, man!" But nowhere in the Bible are
we told to slow down and take it easy.

God's answer for this man was, "You fool! You
will die this very night. Then who will get it all?"
(v. 20 NLT). Jesus concluded his story by saying,
"Yes, a person is a fool to store up earthly wealth but
not have a rich relationship with God." (v. 21 NLT).

Our greatest recreation and rest will come later
in heaven. Meanwhile, we are told to "press on"
(Phil. 3:12), to "not be weary in doing

good" (Gal. 6:9), and to "run the race" (1 Cor. 9:24; Heb. 12:1). Oswald Sanders said, "The world is run by tired men." We never will do great things for God until we have learned to minister when we are tired.

Athletes learn how to press on, even when they are injured. In the same way, God uses people who are willing to work hard and apply themselves.

If more people simply knew these three things, then they would believe in Jesus.

As Paul wrote to the church at Thessalonica, "Don't you remember, dear brothers and sisters, how hard we worked among you? Night and day we toiled to earn a living so that our expenses would not be a burden to anyone there as we preached God's Good News among you" (1 Thess. 2:9). You won't read of any lazy people in the Bible who were used by God, but you will read about many hardworking people who were used by Him.

A LITTLE GOES A LONG WAY

Fifth, if you want to be used by God, then you must share the truth of God with tact and love.

In speaking to the Samaritan woman, Jesus, the Master Evangelist, used something many Christians seriously lack: tact. Jesus appealed to her curiosity and to her inner spiritual thirst:

The woman was surprised, for Jews refuse to have anything to do with Samaritans. She said to Jesus, "You are a Jew, and I am a Samaritan woman. Why are you asking me for a drink?"

Jesus replied, "If you only knew the gift God has for you and who I am, you would ask me, and I would give you living water."

"But sir, you don't have a rope or a bucket," she said, "and this is a very deep well. Where would you get this living water? And besides, are you greater than our ancestor Jacob who gave us this well? How can you offer better water than he and his sons and his cattle enjoyed?"

Jesus replied, "People soon become thirsty again after drinking this water. But the water I give them takes away thirst altogether. It becomes a perpetual spring within them, giving them eternal life."

*"Please, sir," the woman said, "give me some
of that water! Then I'll never be thirsty again,
and I won't have to come here to haul water."*
(John 4:9–15 NLT)

Notice that Jesus did not start out with some
statement like, "Are you saved?" or "Did you know
that you are going to hell?" Nor did He condemn
her with something along the lines of, "Hey, you
harlot! Yeah, you, wicked Jezebel!" No, instead the
Master Communicator showed us how it is to be
done.

This was a dialogue. Jesus spoke, and Jesus
listened. One of the best ways to share your faith
is to listen for awhile to the person with whom you
are speaking. That is what Jesus did. And then He
threw out the bait, so to speak: "If you only knew
the gift God has for you and who I am, you would
ask me, and I would give you living water."
(v. 10 NLT).

LOOKING FOR LOVE

Initially, her response was sarcastic, flippant, and
cynical. In a sense, she was verbally jousting with
Jesus. No doubt this woman was cynical about men
in general. And why wouldn't she be? She probably

was a very attractive woman and had been used and abused by men. But now the men were gone. Her beauty had most likely faded (this was before the advent of cosmetic surgery).

Many young women today think that if they just could be beautiful, then they would be happy and fulfilled. Yet I find it interesting that Halle Berry, regarded as one of the most beautiful women in Hollywood, doesn't seem to agree. She once told an interviewer, "Beauty? Let me tell you something. Being thought of as 'a beautiful woman' has spared me nothing in life. No heartache. No trouble. Love has been difficult. Beauty is essentially meaningless, and it is always transitory." [4]

This Samaritan woman could have said the same thing. She never had found the fulfillment she was looking for in a relationship with a man. As she talked with Jesus, she may have thought, "What is this guy doing? What game is he playing with me? What does he really want?"

But in the course of their conversation, Jesus would point out to her three important facts:

1. Who He was
2. What He had to offer
3. How she could receive it

If more people simply knew these three things, then they would believe in Jesus.

So let's begin with who Jesus was. The woman asked, "Are you greater than our ancestor Jacob who gave us this well? How can you offer better water than he and his sons and his cattle enjoyed?" (v. 12 NLT). Jesus did not tell her about the night that Jacob sent his family and flocks ahead, and how, when Jacob was alone in prayer with God, a mysterious visitor appeared. As Jacob wrestled with the unknown visitor all night, the visitor said, "Let Me go, for the day breaks" (Gen. 32:26).

Jesus could have responded, "Am I greater than Jacob? I wrestled with him—he was a wuss! I knew Moses and Abraham too. Am I greater? I'm their Creator! I'm the One they worshipped!" Had He said this, she would have thought He was insane. She wasn't ready for this spiritual truth yet. And that is an important thing to remember when we share our faith: we should not give people more than they can digest. Remember, the essential gospel is essentially a simple message. As Billy Graham once said, "I study to be simple."

The gospel message is not only what you put in, but it is also what you leave out. After seeing the response to the invitation at a Harvest Crusade or at one of our services at Harvest Christian Fellowship, people have told me they were amazed that someone would respond to such a simple message. But that is the whole idea.

Jesus was telling this woman there was nothing the world had to offer that would quench her spiritual thirst. He said, "People soon become thirsty again after drinking this water. But the water I give them takes away thirst altogether. It becomes a perpetual spring within them, giving them eternal life" (vv. 13–14 NLT).

She had come to the well of relationships five different times, hoping to meet the perfect man who would fulfill all her desires. But her Prince Charming turned into a frog, time and time again. Or so it seemed. Her life was a miserable chain of unfulfilling relationships. She would fall in love with a man, only to lose interest and move on to another. She was disappointed again and again. She knew what it was like to fall in love. She had experienced that sensation again and again: the light-headed euphoria, the butterflies in her stomach, the quickening of her pulse. Although she had fallen in love many times, the Samaritan woman had not found true love. It was simply lust, or so-called "love at first sight," which is not necessarily love at all. What is so remarkable about love at first sight? It is when two people have been looking at each other for years that love becomes remarkable.

If you are married, maybe, like this woman, you have "fallen out of love" with your spouse. When you first saw your future husband or wife, it was all you could think about. You lost your appetite, your mouth went dry, and you were tongue-tied whenever you were around him or her. You literally thought about this person all day long. Those are wonderful feelings.

But would you really want to feel that way about your spouse for the rest of your life? Imagine, after twenty years of marriage, you see your mate at the breakfast table. "Uh, good morning, Honey!

What we want always will seem to be just around the bend.

I don't have an appetite, because I have been thinking about you all night. Wow, my heart sure is beating fast!" That sounds more like a recipe for a heart attack than it does for a lasting marriage. A couple needs to mature in their love.

Remember the first time you rode a bike or drove a car? Remember the exhilaration and excitement? It is not realistic to expect to feel the same way about driving now that you have been doing it for thirty years. In the same way, it is not realistic to want to have that initial, falling-in-love phenomenon every day. It is not something we should desire. In speaking of real love, C. S. Lewis said,

> *Love ... is not merely a feeling, it is a deep unity, maintained by the will and deliberately strengthened by habit; reinforced by (in Christian marriage) the grace which both parents ask, and receive, from God. They can have this love for each other even at those moments when they do not like each other; as you love yourself even when you do not like yourself.*[5]

The love C. S. Lewis spoke of here is the kind that a husband and wife can retain, even when each could easily—if they allowed themselves to—be "in love" with someone else. Being in love first moved them to promise fidelity. This quieter love enables them to keep the promise they made to one another. It is on this love that the engine of marriage is run. Being in love was the explosion that started it all.

THIRSTY AGAIN

This woman had searched, but never found, her heart's desire. What she (and so many like her) did not understand is that she was trying to fill a void in her life that was created by God. That void is loneliness for God. Jesus told this woman, "Whoever drinks of this water will thirst again ..." (v. 13). In fact, this statement could be written over all the wells of life.

We could write it over the well of success: *Whoever drinks of this water will thirst again.* We could write it over the well of pleasure: *Whoever drinks of this water will thirst again.* We could write it over the well of materialism: *Whoever drinks of this water will thirst again.* No matter how much we have, apart from Christ, we will thirst again.

I have had many adventures with diets, including those of the low-carb variety. No matter what I am allowed to eat on a certain diet, I always find myself craving what I cannot have. I have said to my wife after a full meal, "I have a void in my life that only carbs can fill!" I dealt with all of this in my book, *"I'm Going on a Diet Tomorrow" (and Other Lies We Tell Ourselves).*

In the same way, we can have a banquet of all this world has to offer, but we will find ourselves still lacking. What we want always will seem to be just around the bend. For example, when you are growing up, you think, "When I am a teenager, that is when it's going to be great!"

When you are a teen, you think, "I can't wait to get a car! If I could just get that car with custom wheels and a stereo, that would do it!"

Then you start thinking, "When I graduate from high school, then I will be happy."

Next, it is, "When I get my college degree, that will do it."

You move on to, "When I start my career and I am financially independent, I will be happy!"

After that you think, "When I find my soul mate

and we get married, then I will be happy!"

A few years of marriage go by, and you think, "Well, if we just had kids, then I would be fulfilled."

That leads to, "If we could just get these kids to move out of the house, then we could be empty-nesters and be free!"

It never ends. You always will be spiritually thirsty if you drink from the wells of this world. But when Jesus quenches that thirst, you will be satisfied.

LIVING WATER

Now we come to *what* Jesus had to offer: "But the water I give them takes away thirst altogether. It becomes a perpetual spring within them, giving them eternal life" (v. 14 NLT). Jesus spoke of a "perpetual spring," as opposed to water that was stagnant. In addition, He was telling the Samaritan woman that her spiritual thirst would be *completely* satisfied. It also would be *permanently* satisfied.

Finally, Jesus told her how to get it. But something in her life had to be set straight before she could drink of the living water.

"Go and get your husband," Jesus told her. "I don't have a husband," the woman replied. Jesus said, "You're right! You don't have a husband—for you have had five husbands, and you aren't even married to the man you're living with now." (vv. 16–18 NLT)

Jesus forced her to admit her sin, because there can be no conversion without conviction. There can be no forgiveness without repentance.

" 'Sir,' the woman said, 'you must be a prophet. So tell me, why is it that you Jews insist that Jerusalem is the only place of worship, while we Samaritans claim it is here at Mount Gerizim, where our ancestors worshiped?' " (vv. 19–20 NLT). She had never met a man like this before. It was as though He could see right through her façade, her act. Although she believed He was a prophet, she still sought to shake her personal conviction and talk about religion instead. She did not want to come face to face with her personal sin.

This is a typical tactic of someone who is uncomfortable with the gospel. They try to go off on tangents. But Jesus went to the heart of the matter. He set the record straight and got things back on track. "Jesus replied, 'Believe me, the time is coming when it will no longer matter whether you worship the Father here or in Jerusalem …' " (v. 21). He then went on to explain to her the right way and wrong way to worship, which we will explore in the next chapter.

So she told Him, " 'I know the Messiah will come—the one who is called Christ. When he comes, he will explain everything to us' " (v. 25 NLT).

Jesus dropped the bombshell: " 'I am the Messiah!' " (v. 26 NLT). In other words, "You're talkin' to Him, girl!" It would appear that, at this moment, instantaneously, despite her hardness, world-weariness, and emptiness, she believed.

If we want to be used by God to point someone toward faith in Christ, then we would do well to note Jesus' approach to this woman.

He did not come to condemn her. Instead, He lovingly came to a woman whom no one else even cared to talk to.

He spoke of her deepest need, that which drove her to the kind of lifestyle she lived.

He was not sidetracked by unnecessary religious or political discussions.

He kept to the subject and won a soul that
hot afternoon.

The result was that a lonely Samaritan woman
became the first female evangelist recorded in the
New Testament. Leaving her water pot behind,
she ran and told the people of her city, "Come and
meet a man who told me everything I ever did!
Can this be the Messiah?" (v. 29 NLT). Even though
she was just moments old in her newfound faith,
she had to tell others.

WHICH WELL WILL IT BE?

How about you? From what "well" are you seeking
satisfaction right now? Is it the well of pleasure?
Sin may be enjoyable at the time, but the Bible says,
"The wages of sin is death … " (Rom. 6:23).

Is it the well of possessions? Ecclesiastes 5:10
says, "Those who love money will never have
enough. How absurd to think that wealth brings
true happiness!" (NLT).

Or, are you seeking satisfaction from the well
of some perfect relationship? That was the problem

with my mom. She thought what she was looking for could in no way be found in the faith she been raised with. It had to be found somewhere else. She thought it was in men. She thought it was in all of those empty, shallow things the world offers. And sadly, she found out by experience that this was not the case. In the end, she came back. As Jesus said, "Whoever drinks of this water will thirst again" (John 4:13).

There are many out there today just like this searching woman, people who are waiting for someone like you to reach out to them with the life-changing message of the gospel.
Will you make yourself available to the Lord to be used in such a way?

It will change our world for the better—one person at a time.

6 THE WORSHIPPER BY THE WELL

Have you noticed how popular worship music has become? Everywhere you turn, there is worship music. It seems as though almost every Christian band is recording a worship album these days. I think this is great, because I am all for any attempt to honor and glorify God.

But we also want to be careful to keep worship in its proper perspective. Not long ago, I saw a television program—an infomercial, if you will—for a worship product that a company was hoping to get into the hands of television viewers. The program featured the testimonies of people who found new meaning in their lives through worship music. One man talked about his drug addiction and how he had been delivered from drugs because of worship music. A couple whose marriage was in shambles described how worship music saved their marriage. Another person who had lost a loved one talked about how worship music helped make it possible to cope with the loss.

As I was watching this, I thought, "Now wait a second. We are getting the cart before the horse here. Worship music doesn't free a person from the power of an addiction. God does. Worship music doesn't save a marriage. God does. Worship music doesn't heal a heart broken by grief. God does. Worship music is a vehicle whereby we honor and praise God. It is designed to bring us into the presence of God." It was God who worked in the lives of those people on the infomercial. We want to be sure and give glory to whom the glory is due.

EVERYONE IS A WORSHIPPER

We want to make sure we are worshipping God, not worshipping worship, because when you get down to it, everyone worships someone or something. Now, we don't all worship God in heaven, but we all worship, because there is some passion, some god with a small "g," or some belief system that drives us in life. It might be undiluted hedonism. It might be materialism. It might be bowing at the altar of self, but we all worship something or someone. Ecclesiastes 3:11 tells us, "He has made everything beautiful in its time. Also He has put eternity in their hearts, except that no one can find out the work that God does from beginning to end." God has uniquely wired human beings to worship. It has been built into us. But the idea is to worship the true and living God. In fact, the apostle Paul lists worship as one of the three great distinctives of true belief. In Philippians 3:3, Paul mentions that true believers:

- Glory in Christ Jesus,
- Put no confidence in the flesh, and
- Worship by the Spirit of God.

And here in John 4, we will learn that "God is Spirit, and those who worship Him must worship in spirit and truth" (v. 24). But it is important for us to know there is a right and wrong way to worship God. When we watch shows like the Academy Awards and the Grammy Awards, we see certain people suddenly thanking God and referring to their blessings when we normally wouldn't expect them to. Their lives tell a different story, a story of rebellion against God. And we wonder what is going on.

We see this happen with political candidates as well. They are careful to include the phrase, "God bless America," in their speeches and talk about how important faith is in their lives. We see news clips of them attending church services and

---

That is what happens when God is missing in our lives. Someone or something will take His place.

---

carrying Bibles. But my question is: How do they live and vote? Do they acknowledge that life begins at conception and then support abortion on demand? Do they talk about how important the family is and then vote for policies that undermine it, including legislation that supports same-sex marriage?

When these things happen, we have a disconnect. I am not claiming these people are or are not Christians, because that is for God to determine. But at the same time, I remember what Jesus said: "But why do you call Me 'Lord, Lord,' and not do the things which I say?" (Luke 6:46). He also said, "If you love me, you will obey what I command."

(John 14:15 NIV). Many people claim allegiance to God, yet contradict what they are saying by the way they live.

An amazing story in the Old Testament shows us this is nothing new. As the story opens, Moses has led the Israelites out of the bondage of Egypt. They have seen miracle after miracle as God intervened on their behalf and provided for them. Now God has instructed Moses to go up to the mountain and receive His commandments. While Moses is away, his brother Aaron is in charge. Let's pick up our story in Exodus 32:

> *When Moses failed to come back down the mountain right away, the people went to Aaron. "Look," they said, "make us some gods who can lead us. This man Moses, who brought us here from Egypt, has disappeared. We don't know what has happened to him."* (v. 1 NLT)

So Aaron told the people to bring all their gold, and he would make a golden calf for them. The people loved this idea.

> *When Aaron saw how excited the people were about it, he built an altar in front of the calf*

and announced, "Tomorrow there will be a
festival to the Lord!"

So the people got up early the next morning
to sacrifice burnt offerings and peace offerings.
After this, they celebrated with feasting and
drinking, and indulged themselves in pagan
revelry. (vv. 5–6 NLT)

Aaron called this "a festival to the Lord," and
the people gladly went along. It is amazing how
some people can do something the Bible clearly
warns against, and then somehow rationalize it and
think it is okay, even good. By doing their "religious
stuff," the people felt they were free to do what
they wanted. They had given God His worship;
now it was time to party.

So here they were, dancing naked before a
golden calf in this so-called "festival to the Lord,"
when Moses came down from the mountain. In an
attempt to explain, Aaron offered Moses the lamest
excuse ever recorded:

"You yourself know these people and what
a wicked bunch they are. They said to me,
'Make us some gods to lead us, for something
has happened to this man Moses, who led us

out of Egypt.' So I told them, 'Bring me your gold earrings.' When they brought them to me, I threw them into the fire—and out came this calf!" (vv. 22–24 NLT*)*

We might smile at this and even feel a little smug, but is this really any different from going to church, lifting our hands in worship, and then going out and breaking God's commandments left and right? No, it is not. That is the wrong way to worship. And make no mistake about it: there is a *right way* and a *wrong way* to worship.

THE RIGHT WAY TO WORSHIP

Jesus explains the difference. In His conversation with the woman at the well, whom we met in the last chapter, He gives us a great overview of the purpose of worship. She was a Samaritan, lonely and miserable after five failed marriages. She apparently thought that a man was going to meet the deepest needs of her heart, so she had gone from relationship to relationship.

That is what happens when God is missing in our lives. Someone or something will take His place, as Romans 1:21 tells us: "Yes, they knew

God, but they wouldn't worship him as God or even give him thanks. And they began to think up foolish ideas of what God was like. The result was that their minds became dark and confused" (NLT). Failing to glorify God, this woman tried to fill the void with men as she turned to immoral living.

Sadly in our culture today, if a woman has been married and divorced five times, she might be looked upon with admiration or even celebrated. But in Jesus' day, it would be cause for alienation.

Yet Jesus sought her out and engaged her in conversation. And in the process, Jesus identified for this woman what worship really is and what it ought to be. In fact, we learn *where* we should worship, what is *the right way* to worship, and *how* we should worship.

WHERE SHOULD WE WORSHIP?

So first, let's look at what Jesus had to say about where we should worship:

> "Sir," the woman said, "you must be a prophet. So tell me, why is it that you Jews insist that Jerusalem is the only place of worship, while

we Samaritans claim it is here at Mount
Gerizim, where our ancestors worshiped?"
Jesus replied, "Believe me, the time is coming
when it will no longer matter whether you
worship the Father here or in Jerusalem. You
Samaritans know so little about the one you
worship, while we Jews know all about him,
for salvation comes through the Jews."
(vv. 19–22 NLT).

The Samaritan woman was making a big deal
about where God is worshipped, claiming the
Samaritans believe God should be worshipped
at Mount Gerizim. But Jesus brushed it off:

The God we worship must be the true
God—not a god of our own making.

"You Samaritans know so little about the one you
worship, while we Jews know all about him, for
salvation comes through the Jews" (v. 22 NLT).
In other words, "You don't even know what you
are talking about. You are completely missing
the point."

If Jesus had gone into greater detail with her, no doubt He would have pointed out that the Samaritans' worship was flawed, because they used only the first five books of the Bible, thus limiting themselves to an incomplete revelation of who God is. They worshipped in ignorance, and you cannot effectively worship a God you know nothing about.

I read a newspaper article about a group of clerics, neuroscientists, and architects who had joined efforts to study how the mind reacts to the sensation of entering a house of worship. They asserted that the brain responds to certain styles of architecture, allowing for great worship. Dr. Andrew Newberg of the University of Pennsylvania cited his experiments with Franciscan nuns and Buddhist monks who were deep in meditation and how they attained states in which they felt united with a greater spirit or force. The Reverend Patrick Russell, a neuroscientist turned minister, said, "In deeply religious states they find a sense of oneness with the world." [6]

But that is not worship. That is mysticism. I don't want "a sense of oneness with the world," because the Bible tells me not to love the world or the things in the world (see 1 John 2:15). We don't need ornate buildings to worship God. We can be in a cathedral and worship Him. We can be out in an open field and worship Him. And we can be in a little country church with a few boards missing and worship Him. You see, it is not about *where* we worship. It is about *how* we worship and *why* we worship. That is what it comes down to.

Consider some biblical examples of where people worshipped. Paul and Silas were thrown into a dungeon—and I don't mean a prison cell like there is today. This was a cave, a place with no ventilation or sanitation and no windows. Not only were Paul and Silas thrown into this horrible environment, but their backs had been ripped open by a Roman whip. Their feet were fastened in stocks, causing excruciating pain. Yet the Bible says that at midnight, Paul and Silas sang praises to God (see Acts 16:25).

Or how about Jonah? Where was he when he had his worship experience? He was in the belly of a very large fish. How is that for a cathedral?

Daniel worshipped in a lions' den.

So it is not about *where* we worship. It is about

our hearts, our motives, and having a proper
understanding of who God is.

WHAT IS THE RIGHT WAY TO WORSHIP?

This brings us to the question of *what* God
requires in worship. Jesus explained to her, "God
is Spirit, so those who worship him must worship
in spirit and in truth" (v. 24 NLT). With these words,
Jesus indicated the fundamental elements of true
worship. There are two essential ingredients:
1. God must be worshipped in Spirit.
2. God must be worshipped in truth.

Let's start with the latter: God must be
worshipped in truth. This comes back to our
view of God. The God we worship must be the
true God—not a god of our own making. So our
worship of God must be based on truth. And what
is that truth?

*First, God can only be approached and known
though Jesus Christ.* It is through His blood,
and His blood alone, that we have access to God.
Hebrews 10:19–20 says, "And so, dear brothers and
sisters, we can boldly enter heaven's Most
Holy Place because of the blood of Jesus. This is

the new, life-giving way that Christ has opened up for us through the sacred curtain, by means of his death for us (NLT).

Second, God is worthy of our worship, and we should worship him whether or not we feel like it. As Hebrews 13:15 reminds us, "Therefore by Him let us continually offer the sacrifice of praise to God, that is, the fruit of our lips, giving thanks to His name." Do you think Paul and Silas were in the mood to worship there in the dungeon? Would you have been?

Or take Job for example. Talk about a bad day. He lost his possessions. He lost his family. He lost his health. He lost everything. Yet what does the Bible say Job did?

> *Then Job arose, tore his robe, and shaved his head; and he fell to the ground and worshiped. And he said: "Naked I came from my mother's womb, and naked shall I return there. The Lord gave, and the Lord has taken away; blessed be the name of the Lord."*
> *(Job 1:20–21)*

You see, it is one thing to come to church and worship when we feel like it, when things are going reasonably well. The bills are paid. The sun is shining. The birds are singing. The kids are fine. Everything is good. So we say, "Praise God! Let's worship."

The heart of the matter is the matter of the heart.

Then the next Sunday, the sun is not shining. The birds are not singing. The kids are not doing well. There are problems. So we think, "Well, I don't want to worship. I don't feel like it." But that is when we need to worship more than ever. That is when we need to say, "Lord, I am helpless. Lord, I need Your wisdom. I need Your guidance. I need Your power. I need Your comfort. Lord, I am turning to You." We worship regardless of our circumstances, because God is worthy of our praise. We should worship God not because we are in the mood, but because God has asked us to and has everything in control. That is the sacrifice of praise.

Third, God is far more interested in our motives than in our talents. When we worship, we stand before an audience of one. If, in worship, we want people to look at us or we are thinking about something else altogether, that is not worship. God looks on the heart.

Remember Cain and Abel? Both were raised in a godly home. Both heard the Word of God from their youth. Both were no doubt taught to pray and to worship God. But one was a true worshipper, offering an acceptable act of worship. The other was a false worshipper, offering an unacceptable act of worship. One was accepted. The other was rejected. Hebrews 11:4 tells us, "By faith Abel offered to God a more excellent sacrifice than Cain, through which he obtained witness that he was righteous, God testifying of his gifts; and through it he being dead still speaks." The same passage also reminds us, "Without faith it is impossible to please Him … " (v. 6). It all came down to motive—the *why* of worship.

Worship is really a form of prayer, and the sad but amazing thing is that we can sing worship songs to God without even a single thought of Him in the process. As we drone on, we are really thinking, "I don't like this song," or "Look at the outfit that person is wearing," or "I'm hungry," or "It's too cold in here," or "When will this service end?"

But Jesus said, " 'These people draw near to Me with their mouth, and honor Me with their lips, but their heart is far from Me. And in vain they worship Me, teaching as doctrines the commandments of men' " (Matt. 15:8–9).

God is looking on our hearts when we are worshipping. One can stand in a worship service with arms outstretched toward heaven, tears rolling down his or her cheeks, and singing the praises of God with a clear, beautiful, and very loud voice. We may notice someone like that and think, "Now that person is really worshipping!"

Then we may spot someone with hands raised only shoulder-high, if at all, singing quietly—and not very well. We might think, "That person needs to worship more."

But what *is* worship? A lot of it comes down to what is happening in our hearts. There can be a place for outstretched arms as well as quiet voices. As C. H. Spurgeon said, "God does not regard our voices; He hears our hearts. And if our hearts do not sing, we have not sung at all." Jesus told the story of the Pharisee and the tax collector who went to pray (or worship):

*"The Pharisee stood and prayed thus with
himself, 'God, I thank You that I am not like
other men—extortioners, unjust, adulterers,
or even as this tax collector. I fast twice a week;
I give tithes of all that I possess.' And the tax
collector, standing afar off, would not so much
as raise his eyes to heaven, but beat his breast,
saying, 'God, be merciful to me a sinner!' I tell
you, this man went down to his house justified
rather than the other; for everyone who exalts
himself will be humbled, and he who humbles
himself will be exalted." (Luke 18:11–14)*

Sometimes we pray with our lips, but we do not
worship. Sometimes we sing, but we do not worship.
Sometimes we give, but we do not worship. And
sometimes we do none of these things, but we are
in our deepest worship. There are a lot of ways we
can worship God. There are a lot of ways we can
honor His name. After all, the heart of the matter
is the matter of the heart.

*Fourth, we cannot worship God when we
knowingly have sin in our lives.* The psalmist
wrote, "Who may climb the mountain of the Lord?
Who may stand in his holy place? Only those whose

hands and hearts are pure, who do not worship idols and never tell lies." (Ps. 24:3–4 NLT).

Does this mean that I have to be perfect to worship God? Absolutely not. Every one of us sins, and we need to recognize that. We sin knowingly and sometimes in ignorance. That is why Jesus taught us to pray, "Forgive us our sins, just as we have forgiven those who have sinned against us" (Matt. 6:12). It is essentially recognizing the fact that we do sin—many times—even when we do not realize we are sinning.

What it comes down to is the fact that if you knowingly sin against God, then your prayers will not be heard and your worship will not be received. For example, if I know that I am lying to someone and have no plans to stop anytime soon, I cannot expect my worship to be meaningful to God. Or if you are stealing from someone and plan to keep on stealing from that person, then don't expect God to be honored by your worship. We think maybe we can compensate by just singing louder. But God doesn't want us to sing louder. God would rather that we just shut up, to be perfectly frank. God said in Amos 5:23–24, "Away with your hymns of praise!

They are only noise to my ears. I will not listen to your music, no matter how lovely it is. Instead, I want to see a mighty flood of justice, a river of righteous living that will never run dry" (NLT).

So we think, "Well, I will give more in the offering." But God says, "Keep it. It is tainted. I don't want it."

It brings joy to God when we praise Him.

It is not that God doesn't want us to worship or to give to His work. Rather, God wants our lives and our worship to be combined together in an honorable way for Him. God wants us to worship in the right way. And God wants our hearts more than anything else.

HOW SHOULD WE WORSHIP?

So not only are we to worship God in truth, but we are also to worship Him in Spirit: "God is Spirit, and those who worship Him must worship in spirit and truth" (John 4:24). We can be completely orthodox in our beliefs, yet not express our praise toward Almighty God in a passionate way. Yes, our worship of God should be based on truth. We should worship God in a correct way. And yes, our worship of God should engage the mind and intellect. We should know about God clearly. But then our worship of God should engage our affections, our hearts, and our emotions as well.

God can only be approached and known and worshipped through Jesus Christ.

Of course, this does not mean that worship always will be an emotional experience. As I have already pointed out, we must never worship only because we feel like it or because we are in the right mood. But worship will, and should, engage the emotions.

We can be so focused on our emotions and feelings that we worship a god of our own making. At the same time, we can be so focused on our theology that we do not express ourselves to God, and thus become emotionally dead and out of touch.

Think about all the places where we express our emotions: weddings, movie theaters, football games, baseball games, hockey games, political rallies, and concerts to name a few. Yet if we express any emotion in church, some people will look at us and think, "What a fanatic!" But why is it that our emotions cannot be engaged?

One of the ways we can worship God in spirit is by lifting our hands in an expression of praise. We are told in Psalm 63:3–4, "Because Your loving-kindness is better than life, my lips shall praise You. Thus I will bless You while I live; I will lift up my hands in Your name."

Now if someone came up to you with a gun and said, "This is a hold up," you probably would raise both hands. Why? Because you are surrendering. When we lift our hands to God, we are surrendering. We are saying to the Lord that we surrender our lives, our plans, and everything we have to Him. But that is not comfortable for a lot of people. It may seem awkward, but it is something we can do to honor God. And that is one of the ways we can worship Him in spirit.

Notice that in addition to lifted hands, the psalmist also mentions praising lips. Sometimes when believers are worshipping together, certain people will just fold their arms, look around, and not even try. They don't engage. They don't sing. They just look around. "Well," you say, "maybe it's because there are so many songs. There are so many words to learn." But repetition is the way you learn. We need to at least try.

Think of all the data you have stored in your brain that you didn't even try to learn. I have so much worthless information inside my mind it is pathetic. I still know, word for word, songs that I don't ever remember consciously memorizing, such as the theme songs to *The Flintstones* and *The Beverly Hillbillies*. You probably know them too, don't you?

So if we can unconsciously learn the theme songs to television shows, I think it is very possible that we can learn the lyrics to some great worship songs. Why not pick up a worship CD and start listening to it in your car? Why not take advantage of your commute time to listen to Christian radio? Your vehicle can become a sanctuary on wheels—a place for worship, a place for teaching, and a place for learning some new Christian songs.

Remember, it brings joy to God when we praise Him. In fact, we can also please Him by *thinking* about Him. The psalmist said, "May he be pleased by all these thoughts about him, for I rejoice in the Lord" (Ps. 104:34 NLT). And Malachi 3:16 tells us,

Then those who feared the Lord spoke with each other, and the Lord listened to what they said. In his presence, a scroll of remembrance was written to record the names of those who feared him and loved to think about him. (NLT)

The phrase, "the Lord listened," means "to prick the ear, to bend down so as not to miss a single word."

So God wants us to express our worship to Him in spirit and in truth. But it all comes back to this: our entry into God's presence, our access to His throne, is made available because of the death of Jesus Christ on the cross. God can only be approached and known and worshipped through Jesus Christ.

But as I pointed out at the beginning of this chapter, if you are not worshipping the true and living God, then you will worship a god of your own composition or some false god.

In the late 1500s, a Japanese warlord known as Toyotomi Hideyoshi decided that he wanted to create a colossal statue of Buddha to place in the Nanzenji Temple in Kyoto. For five years, fifty thousand workers labored to create this statue. Shortly after its completion, the earthquake of 1596 struck, bringing the roof down on the shrine and ruining the statue. In a rage, Hideyoshi shot an arrow at the fallen Buddha and shouted, "I put you here at great expense, and you can't even look after your own temple!"

That is the problem with a false god. It can't hear you. It can't see you. It is not aware of you. Why? Because it is not real. It is a god of your own making.

But the true God, the living God, not only can take care of a temple, He can take care of you. He sees you. He knows about you. He cares about you. He hears you. He is interested in you.

And that is why we worship Him: because He is worthy. In fact, our word, "worship," comes from an old English word that could be translated "worth-ship." In other words, we worship a God who is worth it. He deserves our praise.

AN APPOINTMENT AT THE POOL

I think we all have thought of questions we would like to ask God someday. When something happens in our lives that seems inexplicable, we wonder, "Why did God allow this to happen?" I am glad the Bible promises us there is coming a day when all of our questions will be answered.

A Sunday School teacher was speaking to her class about this very subject and invited her students to write down their questions for God. Here are some questions the children handed in:

"Did you mean for the giraffe to look like that, or was it an accident?"

"I like the Lord's Prayer best of all. Did you have to write it a lot, or did you get it right the first time? I have to write everything I ever write over again."

There were also some comments and complaints:

"Thank you for the baby brother, but what I prayed for was a puppy!"

"How come you didn't invent any new animals lately? We still just have all the old ones."

"I bet it is very hard for you to love all of everybody in the world. There are only four people in our family and I can never do it."

"We read that Thomas Edison made light. But in Sunday School they said you did it. I bet he stole your idea."

No matter what age we are, it seems we all have some questions for God. But in the pages to follow, I would like for us to consider some questions God has for us. Our answers to these questions will, quite literally, change the course of our lives.

———◦◦◦◦———

I do not think that God's healing power somehow rests at a certain location.

———◦◦◦◦———

One question in particular is found in John 5. It is a question Jesus posed some two thousand years

ago to a hurting, lonely, and isolated man. And it is
a question that He is still asking today. Let's look at
the story together:

> *After this there was a feast of the Jews, and*
> *Jesus went up to Jerusalem. Now there is in*
> *Jerusalem by the Sheep Gate a pool, which*
> *is called in Hebrew, Bethesda, having five*
> *porches. In these lay a great multitude of sick*
> *people, blind, lame, paralyzed, waiting for*
> *the moving of the water. For an angel went*
> *down at a certain time into the pool and*
> *stirred up the water; then whoever stepped*
> *in first, after the stirring of the water, was*
> *made well of whatever disease he had. Now a*
> *certain man was there who had an infirmity*
> *thirty-eight years. When Jesus saw him lying*
> *there, and knew that he already had been in*
> *that condition a long time, He said to him,*
> *"Do you want to be made well?"*
>
> *The sick man answered Him, "Sir, I have*
> *no man to put me into the pool when the water*
> *is stirred up; but while I am coming, another*
> *steps down before me."*

*Jesus said to him, "Rise, take up your bed
and walk." And immediately the man was
made well, took up his bed, and walked.
(John 5:1–8)*

Notice the story begins with an interesting
phrase: "After this … " (v. 1). We often see this
type of wording in the gospels. In Matthew, we see
the word "then" used repeatedly. Mark's Gospel
uses the word, "immediately." Then in Luke, we
read, "It came to pass. … " Here in John's Gospel,
we find the phrase, "after this," used a total of
seven times.

So what is the significance when we see "then,"
"immediately," "it came to pass," and "after this?"
It tells us that Jesus was acting according to a
predetermined plan and purpose. There were no
accidents in His ministry. He had appointments to
keep that had been set long ago in the counsels of
eternity. We have already read about His appointment with Nicodemus at night and His appointment with the Samaritan woman at noon.

WAITING FOR A MIRACLE

Now Jesus has an appointment at the pool. There, a poor, forgotten man with a disability for thirty-eight years was waiting for a healing touch from God. And according to this passage, he apparently believed that touch would come by way of an angel: "For an angel went down at a certain time into the pool and stirred up the water; then whoever stepped in first, after the stirring of the water, was made well of whatever disease he had" (v. 4). Whether this actually happened, we don't know. It is worth noting that this verse is not in all the original manuscripts. While this certainly would be within an angel's power, it does cause one to wonder if this was something an angel of the Lord actually would do. Basically, the healing was on a first-come, first-served basis. If you happened to be close enough and fast enough to step into the water first when the angel allegedly stirred it up, then you would be healed. So whether this was true or whether it was a commonly held belief, we don't know.

Of course, we have the equivalent of this today. Certain legends have grown around certain places. One example is a spa in Lourdes, France, which many people believe has divine healing properties. Another is the shrine of Guadalupe in Mexico City, where people go to find healing power. But is there any truth to these rumors? Personally, I don't think so. I don't think that God's healing power somehow rests at a certain location, and if you go there, then you will be healed.

Many times, I think this is nothing more than a superstition people turn to. We love to believe there is a tangible thing that can somehow make us better. Sometimes it is as simple as a rabbit's foot or a good-luck charm. Maybe it is a lucky jacket, color, or number. It might even be a religious object such as a crucifix that seems to provide some measure of comfort. But a child of God should have no need for religious medals, lucky charms, or any other of these things. Luck plays no part whatsoever in the life of the Christian. To feel a need for these things is really a form of idolatry.

The Christian is guided by Divine Providence,

not the luck of the draw. The slogan of the believer is not *"Que sera, sera,* whatever will be, will be. ... " Rather, it is, "We know that all things work together for good to those who love God, to those who are the called according to His purpose" (Rom. 8:28).

Now I am not saying it is wrong to wear a cross. What I am saying is that if you believe there is some kind of mystical, supernatural power in a particular object, then it is essentially a form of idolatry. The Bible warns against having any other gods other than the one, true God and against having "idols of any kind ... " (Ex. 20:4 NLT). If we need a physical object to help us know a spiritual God, then something is wrong with us and our lives before God. True believers should neither need nor depend on these things.

Having said that, here was a man who believed that if an angel troubled the water, and if he could somehow be the first to get into the water, then he would be healed. He had been waiting for thirty-eight years, unable to move. Perhaps he had been paralyzed by an accident. We do not know. But something happened in his life that brought this about.

WHY BAD THINGS HAPPEN TO GOOD—
AND BAD—PEOPLE

Sometimes we get sick simply because we live in a sin-sick world. Disease, and death in general, were never part of God's original plan. If Adam and Eve had not sinned, there would not be any sickness. There would not be any aging. And most importantly, I would have a full head of hair. But this is all a result of sin in general. We are told in Romans 5:12, "Therefore, just as through one man sin entered the world, and death through sin, and thus death spread to all men, because all sinned."

Not everyone wants to be made well.

However, sometimes we fall ill because of our own personal sin. Paul wrote that some of the members of the Corinthian church had become ill and had even died because of their sin: "For this reason many are weak and sick among you, and many sleep" (1 Cor. 11:30).

Consider the person who has abused alcohol for his entire life. One day, his liver goes out. Is there a connection between the lifestyle he has chosen and what has happened to him physically? Absolutely.

What about someone who goes out on a drunken binge, gets behind the wheel of a car, and is injured in an auto accident? Is there a connection between the way she was living and the horrible thing that happened to her? Of course.

Or how about the person who is sexually immoral? He frequently engages in extramarital sex. Then he discovers he has contracted AIDS. Is there a connection between his lifestyle and this horrible virus he now has? The answer is yes.

So there can be a connection between what we do and what happens to us.

However, I am not asserting that every person who has liver damage, AIDS, or who has been involved in a car accident came into those circumstances because they sinned. But we do need to accept the fact that when we choose to sin, there will be consequences.

Still, there are other times when God will allow sickness in the life of a believer to teach something. For example, when the apostle Paul experienced his "thorn in the flesh," he had not sinned in any way that we know of. In fact, he had recently had a vision of heaven. Yet the Lord allowed this suffering of some kind. Paul asked three times for God to take it away. But His answer was, "My grace is sufficient for you, for My strength is made perfect in weakness" (2 Cor. 12:9). This would suggest that God allows sickness to keep us humble or to teach us. Sometimes He may allow it to bring us back to Him, as we see in Psalm 119:67: "Before I was afflicted I went astray, but now I keep Your word."

Sometimes we are so stubborn and proud that we think we don't need God. Everything is going well. So the Lord will get our attention. Something will happen to wake us up. And suddenly we realize that maybe we do need God after all.

Another thing to consider is the possibility that when God allows sickness in the lives of believers, sometimes the only thing He is waiting for is for us to call out to Him in prayer and ask for His healing touch. I believe God can and does heal people today. As James 4:2 tells us, "You do not have because you do not ask." Have you done that yet? If God says no to your request, then know that His grace will be sufficient to see you through and sustain you.

If He doesn't answer your prayer right away, then ask Him again.

AN UNEXPECTED QUESTION

Out of this crowd of sick and suffering people at the pool called Bethesda, Jesus selected one man. He didn't preach to everyone. He didn't heal everyone. He went to only one individual and asked a poignant question, and in some ways, an unexpected question: "Do you want to be made well?" (v. 6).

Now what kind of question is that to ask a man like this? We would almost expect him to answer, "No. I like hanging out here. This is just a lot of fun. You really ought to join me." He might have thought Jesus was making fun of him. After all, why would someone ask him something like that?

But he did not respond that way. And Jesus was not mocking him either. He was asking a legitimate question. It was an important question, because not everyone wants to be made well. Not everyone wants his or her life to change.

It reminds me of another question God asked in the Garden of Eden after Adam and Eve sinned.

The Lord came walking in the Garden in the cool of the day, calling out to Adam, "Where are you?" (Gen. 3:8). Now why did God call out for Adam? Was God totally oblivious to Adam's whereabouts? Of course not. He knew where Adam was. God called out to Adam because, among other things, it was to convince him of sin. He was not looking for information; He was looking for a confession. He wanted to confront Adam and his wife Eve with their sin so they could set it right and be restored into fellowship with Him. So He was calling out, "Where are you?"

God could ask some of us that question right now: "Where are you?" as in, "Where are you in life? Are you where you ought to be spiritually right now? Are you satisfied with your spiritual condition, or does change need to take place?"

"Do you want to be made well?" Jesus asked this man. In other words, "Do you want to change your life, not just physically, but also spiritually? Are you willing to place yourself, just as you are, in My hands? Are you ready for Me to do for you what you are unable to do for yourself?"

You see, as long as we think we can work it out on our own, as long we think we will figure it out someday, we never will get anywhere. We need to call out to God and say, "Lord, I can't do it on my own, but I am calling out to You and asking You to help me. I am asking You to forgive me." If you will call out to Jesus Christ, then He will forgive you. If you are willing to turn from your sin, make a clean break with the past, and begin to follow Him, then you will see things happen in your life that you never thought were possible.

A marriage that is falling apart can be restored. An addiction that seems too powerful to break can be broken. A behavior pattern can be changed by the power of God. But we have to want it. Do you want to be made well?

God asks this question because He wants us to want His help. You see, not everyone wants to change. Not every person who is a drinker wants to stop. Not every person who uses drugs wants to change their ways. Not every person who is living immorally wants to live God's way. Not every person who steals wants to no longer steal.

In reality, God helps those who cannot help themselves.

Some people are comfortable in their sinful lifestyles. They like where they are. They have grown accustomed to the darkness. Have you ever walked out of a matinee and started squinting in the afternoon sun because you had grown accustomed to the darkness of the movie theater? That is what it is like for people who don't want to change. As Oswald Chambers observed, "Sin enough and you will soon be unconscious of sin."

You can become so accustomed to a lifestyle you have chosen that you really don't want to break free from it. You don't want to change the company you are keeping. You don't want to stop going to the places you have been going. You like where you are. So Jesus asks, "Do you want to change your life?" Your answer, if you were honest, would be, "No, not really. I like where I am."

Where are you today? Are you where you ought to be? Or, do you want to change your life? Do you really want your marriage healed? Do you really

want to be free of your dependency on drugs or
alcohol or both? Do you really want to break free
from sexual sin? If so, then know there is God's
part and there is yours, as we will discover from
this story.

OUT OF OPTIONS

Jesus' honest question brought an honest answer:
"Sir, I have no man to put me into the pool when
the water is stirred up; but while I am coming,
another steps down before me" (v. 7). In other
words, "I have tried everything and it failed. I can't
get there."

I think it was the utter helplessness of this man
that drew Jesus to Him. Perhaps the night before
he had called out to God. Maybe, even on this day,
he moaned a quiet prayer to heaven, not realizing,
in his wildest dreams, that God himself would
personally bring him his answer—not what he
asked for, but something far better.

He wanted an angel to "stir the waters," but
instead God came and stirred up his life, not only
physically, but spiritually as well. The Bible tells

us that God "is able to do exceedingly abundantly above all that we ask or think" (Eph. 3:20).

You may be able to identify with this man. Maybe you feel you are all alone. Maybe you have been divorced or widowed. Maybe you are out on your own in some way, shape, or form. Maybe you recently left home for college, or you are still single. You feel isolated. You understand what this man was going through.

Or maybe, like this man, you know what it is like to be paralyzed by some kind of sin or vice that seems to have a stranglehold on your life right now. You have tried to break free, but you can't.

The group of people at this pool is also a picture of many today: "Now there is in Jerusalem … a pool, which is called in Hebrew, Bethesda, having five porches. In these lay a great multitude of sick people, blind, lame, paralyzed, waiting for the moving of the water" (John 5:2–3). The word, "paralyzed," in verse 3 could be translated, "without strength." Or as another translation puts it, "help-less and powerless." Contrary to popular opinion, the Bible does not teach that God helps those who help themselves. Rather, it says, "For when we were

still without strength, in due time Christ died for
the ungodly" (Rom. 5:6). God tells us that, when
it was impossible to do anything for ourselves spiritually, Christ died for us. So in reality, God helps
those who cannot help themselves. God helps
the helpless.

Many are like this paralyzed man today: "Sir,
I have no man. ... " In other words, "I have no one
to help me." They have given up all hope of change.
They have resigned themselves to their position
in life.

STEPS IN THE RIGHT DIRECTION

So what was Jesus' response to this man, and to
all those who have lost hope?

First, Jesus asked for the impossible. Jesus told
this man to do what he had not been able to do
for thirty-eight years: "Rise, take up your bed and
walk" (v. 8). Now let's understand that when Jesus
gave him the command to take up his bed, it would
not have been of the king-size, four-poster variety.
This man's bed probably consisted of something
like a bedroll, a sleeping bag, or maybe even a
simple straw mat. Jesus was saying, "I want you to

pick that up, and I want you to walk. I want you to do what you have never done before. And if I tell you to do it, then you can do it." As the Scripture reminds us, "Ah, Lord God! Behold, You have made the heavens and the earth by Your great power and outstretched arm. There is nothing too hard for You" (Jer. 32:17).

So when God tells us to live this Christian life, when God tells husbands to love their wives as Christ loves the church, when God tells wives to submit to their husbands as unto the Lord, when God tells children to submit to their parents and obey them, when God tells us to resist temptation, when God tells us to go into all the world and preach the gospel, then it can be done. Otherwise, He would not have commanded us to do these things.

Now we cannot do them in our own strength. But we can do them in His strength. According to Philippians 4:13, "[We] can do all things through Christ who strengthens [us]." And as I have often said, the calling of God is the enabling of God.

Second, Jesus removed all possibility of a relapse. Jesus told this man to take up his bed and walk. In other words, Jesus was saying,

"There is no backup plan here, Buddy. If this doesn't work out, you won't go to your little bed anymore.

Have you burned the bridge?

That is over with. That is the past. We are moving forward. You can walk now. This is a whole new world for you."

When God calls us to do something, He expects us to make a break from the past. We see this in the Old Testament story of Elijah and Elisha.

When Elijah was looking for a successor, the Lord told him that it was to be Elisha. One day Elijah saw Elisha plowing a field with a team of oxen. Elijah went over and threw his mantle around Elisha's shoulders, which was a symbolic gesture that said, "You are my successor. You are to carry on my ministry."

Elisha's response was, "First let me go and kiss my father and mother good-bye, and then I will go with you!"

But Elijah told him, "Go on back! But consider what I have done to you." (1 Kings 19:20 NLT).

Elijah was saying, "If you don't get what is happening right now, if you think you have time to think about it, then just forget about it."

But Elisha understood immediately and wanted to indicate that to the prophet. So Elisha made a bonfire out of his plowing rig. Then the oxen became filet mignon as the two prophets had some nice barbecue together.

That is called burning your bridges. And that is what many Christians have failed to do. They have said, "Yes, I want to follow the Lord," but they never remove the possibility of a relapse. They haven't made a break with their old lifestyle. They haven't made a break with past relationships. They haven't made a break with their sinful vices. As a result, these things still have a hold on them and they are not moving forward spiritually.

But God asks the impossible. He asks us to have no conditions for a relapse—no backup plan.

In 1990 when we were holding our first crusade at the Pacific Amphitheater, a drug dealer came forward on one of the first nights during the invitation. He turned in his pager, because that is how he conducted his drug deals. (Cell phones were

not as widely used back then as they are today.)
The next day, the follow-up counselor called him
to see how he was doing.

He told him, "Well, I was out mowing the
grass."

"Oh, you are doing a little yard work?" the
counselor asked.

He said, "No, I was actually mowing down
marijuana plants." This man was burning his
bridges—or mowing them down, if you will.
He was leaving no room for a relapse.

For some Christians, the struggle may be with
alcohol. The first question I would ask is: Do you
have any alcohol left in your house? Why not get
rid of it? Why not pour it down the drain?

Still others may struggle with impure thoughts.
Are there any pornographic magazines laying
around? Get rid of them. Do you have a filtered
Internet service? Get one.

Whatever it is you may be struggling with, my
question is: Have you burned the bridge? Have
you removed the thing you can go back to? That
is what Jesus asked of this man. And that is what
He asks of you.

Jesus doesn't "work" for some, but not for others.

Third, Jesus expected continued success. Jesus told him to take up his bed and *walk*. "Don't expect to get carried," was the implication. "Get on your feet and walk."

Some people say, "Well, I have tried Christianity, but it didn't work for me." But we are not dealing with an it. We are dealing with a Him. Christianity is Christ, and He will work in the life of any man, woman, or child who honestly comes to Him.

It would be like having a friend of mine say to me, "Well, Greg, I tried the whole health club thing and it didn't work for me."

"Really?"

"Oh, yeah. I tried it."

"So you joined a health club?"

"Oh, yeah. Absolutely."

"How long did you go?"

"For a month."

"You went for a month? And you didn't see any improvement?"

"Not one bit of improvement. In fact, I put on weight."

"Really? Well, what did you do at the health club?"

"I just sat around and ate doughnuts."

Although my friend joined a health club, he didn't do what he needed to do. He didn't really do his part. Saying that he tried a health club but that it didn't work for him is not an accurate assessment of what happened. The truth is, he didn't really try.

So when people say, "Oh, tried the Christian thing and it didn't work," I would have to question whether they did their part. I would have a few questions for them.

1. *Did you begin to study and memorize Scripture after you were supposedly converted?*

   The Bible says, "Be diligent to present yourself approved to God, a worker who does not need to be ashamed, rightly dividing the word of truth" (2 Tim. 2:15). Did you study the Bible? As the psalmist wrote in Psalm 119:11, "Your word I have hidden in my heart, that I might not sin against You." Did you memorize Scripture?

2. *Did you get involved in a church on a regular basis?*

Hebrews 10:25 says, "And let us not neglect our meeting together, as some people do, but encourage and warn each other, especially now that the day of his coming back again is drawing near" (NLT).

One Sunday morning after the first service at Harvest Christian Fellowship, I was answering phones for our television program. A woman called to order a CD that we were offering, so I took down her name and information. It turned out that she lived in a city near Riverside, where our church is located, so I asked her where she attended church.

"I go to Harvest Christian Fellowship," she told me.

I said, "It's Sunday. Why aren't you here?"

Sounding a little embarrassed, she offered a not-so-convincing explanation.

I said, "Well, you ought to be here. You can still come to the third service. By the way, this is Pastor Greg." She didn't believe me. So we talked a little bit more. Then I said, "Really, this is Greg Laurie, and I would like to see you at church."

"It really is you!!" she said. "I recognize your voice now! I can't believe I am talking to you, telling you that I wasn't at church today!"

Although I was having a little fun with this unsuspecting caller, my point was that we, as Christians, need to be in regular, consistent fellowship in a local, Bible-teaching church.

3. *Did you get baptized?*

While baptism is not required for salvation, the Bible does command us to be baptized (see Matt. 3:13–16; Matt. 28:19–20; Acts 2:38). So why not obey the Lord in this area?

4. *Did you turn from all known sin?*

The psalmist said, "If I regard iniquity in my heart, the Lord will not hear (Ps. 66:18).

5. *Did you develop a prayer life?*

The Bible tells us to "pray without ceasing, in everything give thanks; for this is the will of God in Christ Jesus for you" (1 Thess. 5:17–18).

6. *Did you deny yourself, take up the cross, and follow Jesus?*

Jesus said, "If anyone desires to come after

Me, let him deny himself, and take up his
cross, and follow Me. For whoever desires
to save his life will lose it, but whoever
loses his life for My sake will find it"
(Matt. 16:24–25).

My question to those who say they have tried
Christianity is: Did you do these things I have just
described? If not, then don't say that you have tried
Christianity. You need to do your part. You see,
Jesus doesn't "work" for some, but not for others.
He will change any person who comes to Him,
just as they are.

So, do you want to change your life? If your
answer is yes, then here is what you need to do:
Expect the impossible. Make no provision for
a relapse. And remember that Jesus expects
continued success.

OUR DATE WITH
DESTINY

8

British novelist William Boyd wrote, "We all want to be happy and we are all going to die. ... You might say these are the only two unchallengeably true facts that apply to every human being on this planet."[1]

Death is a harsh reality that we all will have to deal with sooner or later. And death is no respecter of persons. It does not matter whether you are a billionaire or the poorest of the poor, whether you are an older person or a very young person, or whether you are a president, king, queen, actor, or rock star. Everyone eventually dies.

But then what?

In August 2002, *Newsweek's* cover story, "Why We Need Heaven," offered some interesting information about Americans' view toward their eternal destination—if they think they have one, that is. This article revealed that 76 percent of Americans believe in heaven, while 71 percent believe it is an actual place. The article went on to say that for more than two thousand years, everyone from theologians to children have been asking the same unanswerable questions: Do we keep our bodies in heaven? Are we reunited with loved ones? How do you get there?

The article pointed out that most of us have ceased to correlate specific behaviors with rewards in heaven, but we still think that if we are good, we will go there. Seventy-five percent of Americans believe their actions on Earth determine whether they will get to heaven.[8]

LET'S FACE THE FACTS

Let me say that those so-called "unanswerable" questions are answerable, and we will deal with them a little later in this chapter. But first, I want to address another question: Why do we have to die in the first place? After all, we don't want to face the fact that we are mere mortals, that our days are numbered.

Long ago, in a Garden called Eden, our first parents Adam and Eve disobeyed God and ate the forbidden fruit. God told Adam, "Of every tree of the garden you may freely eat; but of the tree of

the knowledge of good and evil you shall not eat,
for in the day that you eat of it you shall surely die"
(Gen. 2:16–17). And of course, you know the rest
of the story. It was the bite heard around the world,
and we continue to feel its effects to this very day.
The repercussion of Adam and Eve's choice was
the entrance of sin into the world. And as I have
already mentioned, that included things like illness
and the process of aging. These bodies of ours now
wear out and break down with the passing of time.
Wrinkles begin to form.

Of course, a lot of people don't like to accept
the natural process of aging. They are looking for
that elusive fountain of youth. Today, one in three
adults under the age of 50 are now shopping for
unconventional medical treatments. They are
spending more than ten billion dollars a year on
the latest vitamins, potions, and lotions to turn
back the clock. That is not to mention the millions
spent ever year by Americans for cosmetic surgery
in their quest to regain their lost youth. But it is not
going to work.

There is coming a day when we will die, and
there is nothing we can do to change that date with
destiny. As surely as there was a day determined for

each of us to be born, there is a day determined for each of us to die (unless the Rapture comes first, of course). Ecclesiastes 3:1–2 tells us, "To everything there is a season, a time for every purpose under heaven: A time to be born, and a time to die. ... "

There is nothing we can do to postpone our appointment with eternity. But having said that, I want to point out that the real you, your soul, will live forever. Yes, your body will cease to exist, but your soul will live on. That is true of both the believer and the unbeliever, by the way. Everyone is immortal in that sense. Everyone lives on forever. And according the Bible, we will live on in one of two destinations: heaven or hell.

WHERE DO WE GO FROM HERE?

But getting back to our first question: What happens when death takes place? Jesus answers that for us in John 5:

> *Most assuredly, I say to you, the hour is coming, and now is, when the dead will hear the voice of the Son of God; and those who hear will live. For as the Father has life in*

*Himself, so He has granted the Son to have
life in Himself, and has given Him authority
to execute judgment also, because He is the
Son of Man. Do not marvel at this; for the
hour is coming in which all who are in the
graves will hear His voice and come forth—
those who have done good, to the resurrection of life, and those who have done evil, to
the resurrection of condemnation.*
(*vv. 25–29*)

---

*Every wrong ever committed
ultimately will be paid for.*

First, death is not the end of existence. As I
have already pointed out, human beings are eternal
creatures, meaning that our souls live on forever.
Some teach that we simply cease to exist at death.
But the Bible teaches that we live on.

Second, there is a final judgment. This is not
something we hear enough about from our pulpits
these days. I rarely hear a pastor mention hell or
judgment. The apostle Paul, however, was one
preacher who was not afraid to bring this up.

*"Truly, these times of ignorance God over-
looked, but now commands all men everywhere to repent, because He has appointed
a day on which He will judge the world in
righteousness by the Man whom He has
ordained. He has given assurance of this to
all by raising Him from the dead." (Acts 17:30)*

I am not suggesting that hell and judgment
should always be the focus of our sermons. But we
would do well to remember they are clearly taught
throughout Scripture. There is a future judgment.
The Bible tells us that many times.

Also, Jesus gave this sobering warning in
Matthew 12:36: "But I say to you that for every
idle word men may speak, they will give account
of it in the day of judgment."

PROOF THAT GOD IS FAIR

I realize that some people don't like to hear this,
because they don't believe in a God of judgment.
"I believe in a God of love, of mercy, and of compassion," they say. Well, let me just say that I do too.
But really, you do not want to believe in a God who
is not just. You would not want to believe in a God

who merely demonstrates love and compassion, but fails to execute justice and righteousness.

The fact there is a future judgment assures us that ultimately, God is fair. The teaching of a future judgment should satisfy our inward sense of a need for justice in this world. We have all seen things that seem appallingly unjust, and we say to God, "How can they get away with that?" The horrific crimes we hear of in the news desperately show the need for justice in the world. But know this: God is in control, and He keeps very accurate records. The Bible says, "But he who does wrong will be repaid for what he has done, and there is no partiality" (Col. 3:25). Some may escape "the long arm of the law," so to speak, but they never will escape from the God who sees and knows everything.

The teaching of a future judgment frees us from the need to hold grudges and seek revenge. It is not up to us to take vengeance on those who have wronged us, or even to want to do so, because God Almighty has reserved that right for himself. Romans 12:19 reminds us, "Beloved, do not avenge yourselves, but rather give place to wrath; for it is

written, 'Vengeance is Mine, I will repay,' says the
Lord." Every wrong ever committed ultimately will
be paid for. It will be paid when the offender has
repented of his sins and put his faith in Jesus Christ,
who died on the cross for our sins. Or, it will be paid
at the final judgment for those who do not trust in
Jesus for salvation. God will avenge all wrongs that
have been done in this world. The Bible tells us that
in that final day, God will execute His judgment.
Therefore, it is not for us to try to do it.

Jesus gave us the example to follow, as the Bible
tells us: "He never sinned, and he never deceived
anyone. He did not retaliate when he was insulted.
When he suffered, he did not threaten to get even.
He left his case in the hands of God, who always
judges fairly" (1 Peter 2:22–23 NLT).

TWO RESURRECTIONS

Returning to our passage in John 5, we read of
two forms of existence beyond the grave: "Do not
marvel at this; for the hour is coming in which all
who are in the graves will hear His voice and come
forth—those who have done good, to the resurrection of life, and those who have done evil, to

the resurrection of condemnation" (vv. 28–29). According to these verses, there are two resurrections:

1. The resurrection of life, which is for the believer
2. The resurrection of condemnation, which is for the unbeliever

Let's look at another passage that deals with this subject further:

> *Then I saw the souls of those who had been beheaded for their witness to Jesus and for the word of God, who had not worshiped the beast or his image, and had not received his mark on their foreheads or on their hands. And they lived and reigned with Christ for a thousand years. But the rest of the dead did not live again until the thousand years were finished. This is the first resurrection. Blessed and holy is he who has part in the first resurrection. Over such the second death has no power, but they shall be priests of God and of Christ, and shall reign with Him a thousand years. (Rev. 20:4–6)*

The first resurrection is the one all true believers will experience. Believers, meaning those who have put their faith in Jesus Christ, will go immediately into His presence. There will be no layovers. It is a direct flight, so to speak. When a Christian dies, he or she goes straight to heaven. As Jesus said to the thief on the cross, "Today you will be with Me in Paradise" (Luke 23:43).

Think of the purest joy on earth, then multiply that a thousand times, and you may get a fleeting glimpse of heaven's euphoria.

The apostle Paul spoke of his dilemma in which he longed to be in heaven with Jesus, yet realized there was still work for him to do on Earth. He said,

> *For to me, to live is Christ, and to die is gain. But if I live on in the flesh, this will mean fruit from my labor; yet what I shall choose I cannot tell. For I am hard-pressed between the two, having a desire to depart and be with Christ, which is far better. (Phil. 1:21–23)*

Paul spoke of his desire "to depart and be with
Christ" (v. 23). Notice that he did not say, "I am
hard-pressed ... having a desire to depart for a
few thousand years in a state of suspended anima-
tion," or "I am hard-pressed ... having a desire to
depart for purgatory." Paul was clearly stating that
a believer is either at home in the body or is with
the Lord.

This brings us to some of the "unanswerable"
questions, such as: Do we keep our bodies in
heaven? The answer is yes. And no. We will have
new bodies in heaven, but they will not be in the
same state as they are now. According to
1 Corinthians 15:42–43, "Our earthly bodies,
which die and decay, will be different when they
are resurrected, for they will never die. Our bodies
now disappoint us, but when they are raised, they
will be full of glory. They are weak now, but when
they are raised, they will be full of power" (NLT).
This means that if you were disabled on Earth,
you won't be in heaven. If your body has cancer,
or is simply worn out with age, that won't be the
case in heaven.

SOMETHING TO LOOK FORWARD TO

We often talk about the differences there will be when we make our transition from Earth to heaven. But there will be a few similarities too. Heaven is the earthly life of the believer, glorified and perfected. When we pass over to the other side, our minds and our memories will be clearer than ever before. This is great to know, because our memories fade with the passing of time. We forget things, like the names of people we've met, where we parked our car, or where we put our keys.

After returning home from a trip to England awhile back, Cathe and I were experiencing severe jet lag. We arrived home and were planning to go out and have some dinner, but Cathe wanted to wash some clothes first. So she did some laundry and then we left. What she didn't realize was that she had left the faucet running in our laundry room sink, and when we came home about an hour later, we found two to three inches of water all over the floor. It totally destroyed our kitchen floor and even went into some other rooms.

I kind of let it go and didn't really say anything to Cathe. But then a couple of weeks went by, and one day in conversation, I brought up the subject of the modern-day flood.

Cathe said, "Well, you know what? You left the iron on the other day. You actually had the iron on the pad and left it on, and I found it. You could have burned the house down. Flooding the floor is not as bad as burning the house down."

I said, "You know, maybe we can work together. I will start the fire upstairs and you will flood the house downstairs. We will come home, and everything will be just fine."

She laughed at that.

Thankfully in heaven, our memories will work better than ever.

Also, we will know one another in heaven. I think a good example of this is when Jesus was transfigured (see Matt. 17:1–9; Mark 9:2–9; Luke 9:28–36). On each side of Him were Moses and Elijah. Three of the disciples recognized these two prophets. Apparently there were some distinguishing physical characteristic that identified these ancient prophets for them.

In heaven, there will be intuitive knowledge, because our minds will be redeemed from the limitations sin has imposed on them. Although we will not know everything (that knowledge only belongs to God), we will know fully, as the Bible promises:

> *"Now we see but a poor reflection as in a*
> *mirror; then we shall see face to face. Now I*
> *know in part; then I shall know fully, even as*
> *I am fully known" (1 Corinthians 13:12 NIV).*

Think of the purest joy on earth, then multiply that one thousand times, and you may get a fleeting glimpse of heaven's euphoria. This is why David wrote, "In Your presence is fullness of joy; at Your right hand are pleasures forevermore" (Ps. 16:11).

A LONG-AWAITED REUNION

This brings us to another question: Will we be reunited with our loved in heaven? The apostle Paul wrote these words to reassure the Thessalonians about their Christian loved ones who had died.

> *For this we say to you by the word of the*
> *Lord, that we who are alive and remain until*
> *the coming of the Lord will by no means*
> *precede those who are asleep. For the Lord*
> *Himself will descend from heaven with a*
> *shout, with the voice of an archangel, and*

*with the trumpet of God. And the dead in
Christ will rise first. Then we who are alive
and remain shall be caught up together with
them in the clouds to meet the Lord in the air.
And thus we shall always be with the Lord.*
(1 Thess.4:15–17)

The Thessalonian believers were afraid they
would never see their departed loved ones again.
But Paul pointed out that the Rapture would be a
reunion in heaven. We will not only meet the Lord
in the Rapture, but we also will be reunited with
our friends and loved ones who already have gone
on to meet the Lord. David, in speaking of his
child that had died, said, "Can I bring him back
again? I shall go to him, but he shall not return to
me" (2 Sam. 12:23). Mothers and fathers will be
reunited with sons and daughters. Children will
be reunited with their parents. Husbands will be
reunited with wives. Friends will be reunited with
friends. Only the Christian has this hope.

One moment we will be going about our life
here on Earth; the next moment we will be hurtled
into the presence of departed loved ones. And
above all, we will have a face-to-face meeting

with the One whose death in our place made it all happen.

The phrase, "shall be caught up together with them," from verse 17 is a great statement of encouragement. Although death is the great separator, Jesus Christ is the great Reconciler. For the believer, death means a family reunion.

God does not overlook even the smallest, most insignificant gesture on behalf of His kingdom.

So don't ever feel bad for anyone who has died and gone to heaven, because he or she has it far better than you have it right now. Certainly you can miss your friends and loved ones. You might even have deep sorrow about the way in which they died. But don't ever feel bad for them personally. They are happier now than they ever have been—and you will be too when you get to heaven. It is the future destination of all followers of Jesus Christ.

You may be reunited with Christian friends and loved ones by death, or it also could be by the Rapture. The Bible tells us there is a generation that will not see death. In a moment, in the twinkling of an eye, they will be caught up to meet the Lord in the air (see 1 Cor. 15:51–52). The twinkling of an eye is faster than the blinking of the eye. It is like a nanosecond, hardly measurable in human time. That is why the Bible tells us to watch and be ready, because we do not know the day or the hour of the Lord's coming (see Matt. 25:13).

WHEN IT ALL PAYS OFF

It would also appear that we will be reunited with those whom we helped lead to Christ. The apostle Paul, in speaking of the Thessalonians to whom he had ministered, said, "For what is our hope, or joy, or crown of rejoicing? Is it not even you in the presence of our Lord Jesus Christ at His coming?" (1 Thess. 2:19, emphasis mine). Here Paul is saying that these spiritual children of his will one day be his crown of rejoicing when Christ returns. From this, it would appear that each of us would have grouped around us those whom we have helped to believe in Jesus. So if you ever have had the privilege of leading someone to the Lord, then you will have some connection to him or her in heaven.

"Well, I don't know that I have led that many people to the Lord," you may be thinking. Don't be too hard on yourself. The Bible tells us, "So then neither he who plants is anything, nor he who waters, but God who gives the increase" (1 Cor. 3:7). Through your faithful witness, you may have impacted more people than you will ever know. All you need to do is make sure you are faithful with the opportunities God gives you.

When you get to heaven, you will have those people around you whom you have impacted through your witness for Christ. Doesn't that make you want to redouble your efforts? To see even one person standing in heaven before our Savior because you were faithful to share the gospel—that would be worth it all. All the mockery, laughter, and rejection you experience as you try to share the gospel will be worth it for those valuable souls in heaven.

All of this makes heaven more precious and death less frightening. It causes us to long for it, even to be homesick for a place we have never been—almost like a homing instinct that many animals have.

I read a newspaper article about a homing device that was placed on a great white shark that made its way from California to Hawaii and back again. Scientists were amazed this shark had the ability to do that. Think of the sophisticated technology that an average airliner would require to fly from Los Angeles to Hawaii and back. Meanwhile, here was a great white shark, just cruising along, knowing exactly where he was going.

What a tragedy to discover that a person has largely wasted his or her life.

One day you and I will arrive home too—to heaven. And in addition to experiencing a reunion with Christian friends and family members, in addition to being surrounded by those we have helped lead to Christ, we will experience a judgment. As Christians, we will stand before the judgment seat of Christ. This judgment will be different from the judgment for nonbelievers, which is called the Great White Throne Judgment. At that judgment, there is no reprieve. There is no bargaining.

Tragically, for those who end up there, it is too late, because the Great White Throne Judgment will be final. But there is also a judgment for Christians. However, this judgment is not about whether a person will go to heaven, because the fact is that it takes place in heaven. This is a judgment where rewards are given out.

Over the years, many of us have acquired the great awards this world has to offer. Perhaps you have excelled in sports, and your shelves are lined with trophies, plaques, and ribbons. (Growing up, I always received Honorable Mention ribbons, which means that I basically showed up, but lost.)

So when we think of a judgment for Christians, we ought to think of the Olympic ceremonies, for example. Even to compete as an Olympic athlete is a great feat. Frankly, if I qualified for the Olympics and didn't even win a bronze medal, I would be happy to simply say that I had competed in the Olympics. To actually medal would be even more incredible. So the idea is that you are in the Olympics, yes, but only some are going to win the gold, the silver, and the bronze.

In heaven, there will be many rewards for those who have been faithful to God over the years. God does not overlook even the smallest, most insignificant gesture on behalf of His kingdom. Jesus said that our service to God, though not seen by people, is seen by God: "Your Father who sees in secret will reward you openly" (Matt. 6:6). Speaking of this day in the future for all believers, the Bible says, "For we must all appear before the judgment seat of Christ, that each one may receive the things done in the body, according to what he has done, whether good or bad" (2 Cor. 5:10). This same concept is further developed in 1 Cor. 3:11–15:

> *For no one can lay any foundation other than the one already laid, which is Jesus Christ. If any man builds on this foundation using gold, silver, costly stones, wood, hay or straw, his work will be shown for what it is, because the Day will bring it to light. It will be revealed with fire, and the fire will test the quality of each man's work. If what he has built survives, he will receive his reward. If it is burned up, he will suffer loss; he himself will be saved, but only as one escaping through the flames. (NIV)*

This judgment is known as the Bema seat, or
the judgment seat of Christ. The "wood, hay, or
straw" to which verse 15 refers is speaking not so
much of gross sin as it is of putting more importance on the passing things of this world than
on the things of God. It might be a career, sport,
hobby, television, or something else that will one
day pass away. At the judgment seat of Christ, He
will want to know what you did with your time,
what you did with your resources, and what you
did with your opportunities. He will want to know
what you did with the gospel with which you have
been entrusted.

According to this and other passages, our presence in the Kingdom is guaranteed by the promises of God. But our position in the Kingdom will
be won or lost by the quality of service we render
here and now. God will not hold you accountable
for what He has called me to do. And He will not
hold me accountable for what He has called you to
do. But He will hold you accountable as a Christian
who was purchased with His blood at the cross of
Calvary. Salvation is a gift through faith in Jesus
Christ; honor is a reward for service to Jesus Christ.

MAKE IT COUNT

You may think, "Well, I don't really care about rewards. I am just happy to be in heaven." But how tragic to come empty-handed before the One who had His hands pierced for you. How sad it would be to have Jesus say, "Well, what have you done with your life?"

"Well, I'll tell You what. I didn't do much with it, Lord. I was kind of into me. And by the way, I wanted to thank You for purchasing my salvation. I really do appreciate that. But I didn't really do anything for You."

How much better to say, "Well, Lord, I didn't do as much as I could have done, but I did some things. And I did them for Your glory. I offer them to You as my worship and my praise. There is no way that this even comes close to equaling what You did for me, but it is my way of just saying 'thank you' for letting me into heaven in the first place." The apostle Peter said that he wanted to have an abundant entrance into the kingdom of God (see 2 Peter 1:11).

I have done a lot of funeral services over the years for people I knew and people I did not know, both for Christians and non-Christians. The most difficult have been the services for those who did not know the Lord, because I have had very little hope to offer, if any. I could only hope and pray that maybe in the last moments of his or her life, that person trusted Christ.

> ## *It is not about living a good or a bad life.*

During a funeral service, I will, of course, want to talk about some good qualities of a person's life. I do not stand up and say, "You know, George made so much money. Do you know how much money is in his bank account right now?" Although that may have been the most important thing to George while he was on Earth, no one will want to hear that at his memorial service. It would be very inappropriate even to bring it up. Nor would I say, "You know, George was one of the best-looking guys I have ever seen. He was so handsome." George is gone, so that doesn't matter.

What people want to hear at memorial services are endearing traits of the person, some sacrificial act, something about his or her character or nature that indicated goodness, compassion, and so forth.

But how sad it is when I find nothing of the kind, nothing of substance to point to. As the prophet Daniel said to the irreverent King Belshazzar, "You have been weighed in the balances, and found wanting" (Dan. 5:27). In other words, "Belshazzar, you are a spiritual lightweight. You have no substance. And guess what? Your life is required of you!"

What a tragedy to discover that a person has largely wasted his or her life. And it happens far too often.

Imagine what would happen if we really told the truth at funerals. What if the pastor said of the deceased, "He wasted his life pursuing a bunch of stuff that his family will now fight over"? Or, "She was selfish, never spent time with her family, and was dishonest too." Of course, we would be horrified to hear something like that at a funeral. But for some people, these would be accurate statements.

One day, someone will conduct your memorial service, your funeral. What would you want people to say? Would you want them to say, "She really lived for the Lord. Her life really touched mine," or "The world is a better place because he lived here. My life is better off because I met him."

How we live our lives is important, because one day, our lives will end, the eulogy will be given, and the inscription will be made on the tombstone.

When mob boss John Gotti died, the florists of Queens reportedly delivered floral displays that included a six-foot replica of a martini glass, a racehorse, a royal flush, and a Cuban cigar. These supposedly were the things that Gotti's life was about.

What if your friends and family were to have someone design a few floral representations of your life? What would they be? Maybe a Bible? A television set? A football? A golf club? What is your life about? Can you think of a few icons that would symbolize it? What would you want to be remembered for? What will you be remembered for?

These are important things to think about, because one day, your life will end. So make it count. Use it for the glory of God.

SO HOW DO WE GET THERE?

There was one, final, so-called "unanswerable" question raised in *Newsweek's* article that I would like to answer: How do you get to heaven?

If you are a believer reading this, then you already know the answer. But if you are not a believer, then let me tell you. The only way that a person gets into heaven is through Jesus Christ. Jesus said, "I am the way, the truth, and the life. No one comes to the Father except through Me" (John 14:6). There is no other way.

It is not about living a good or a bad life. Even if you have lived a bad life, if you, in your final moments on Earth, call out to Jesus for His forgiveness and truly repent of your sin, then I am telling you that God would forgive you.

And even if you lived the best life, the most commendable life imaginable without Christ, and you did not accept His offer of forgiveness, then you would still face judgment. You can be forgiven, and you can have the guaranteed hope that when you die, you will go to heaven. If you don't have that hope, then don't let another day go by without it.

If you want make sure you are going to heaven, if you are ready to put your trust in Christ and receive His offer to be forgiven of your sins, then will you take a moment to pray this prayer?

Lord Jesus, I know I am a sinner. But I thank
You for dying on the cross and shedding your

blood for my sin. I turn from that sin, and I choose to follow You. Be my Savior. Be my Lord. Be my God. Be my Friend. I want to go to heaven when I die. I want to be ready for Your return. In Jesus' name I pray. Amen.

If you prayed that prayer and meant it, then Jesus Christ has come to live in your heart. To help you grow in your newfound faith, be sure to spend time regularly reading the Bible, praying, going to church, and sharing your faith in Christ with others.

And to help you learn more about what it means to be a follower of Jesus Christ, please visit www.harvest.org/knowgod/.

Notes

1. R. Kent Hughes, John: *That You May Believe* (Wheaton, Ill.: Good News Publishers / Crossway Books, 1999), 17

2. Dale Buss, "Houses of Worship: Christian Teens? Not Very," Taste, *Weekend Journal*, July 9, 2004.

3. Ibid.

4. John Ma, "Actress Halle Berry Says 'Beauty' is Meaningless," *The Christian Post*, August 3, 2004. http://www.christianpost.com/ article/culture/1035/full/actress.halle.berry. says.beauty.is.meaningless/1.htm.

5. C. S. Lewis, *Mere Christianity* (New York: HarperCollins, 2001), 109.

6. Ken Kusmer, The Associated Press, "Divine Design: Architects, clerics look at connection between design and devotion," July 30, 2004. http://www.tdn.com/ articles/2004/07/31/this_day/news01.txt.

7. Bartleby.com, s.v. "8037. Boyd, William. *The Columbia World of Quotations*. 1996," http://www.bartleby.com/66/37/8037 (accessed June 24, 2005).

Notes

8. Lisa Miller with Dan Ephron and Joanna Chen; Anne Underwood, Julie Scelfo, and Margaret Williams, "Why We Need Heaven," *Newsweek*, August 12, 2002

About the Author

Greg Laurie is the pastor of Harvest Christian Fellowship (one of America's largest churches) in Riverside, California. He is the author of over thirty books, including the Gold Medallion Award winner, *The Upside-Down Church,* as well as *Every Day with Jesus* and *Losers and Winners, Saints and Sinners.* You can find his study notes in the *New Believer's Bible* and the *Seeker's Bible.* Host of the *Harvest: Greg Laurie* television program and the nationally syndicated radio program, *A New Beginning,* Greg Laurie is also the founder and featured speaker for Harvest Crusades—contemporary, large-scale evangelistic outreaches, which local churches organize nationally and internationally. He and his wife Cathe have two children and live in Southern California.

Other AllenDavid books
published by Kerygma Publishing

The Great
Compromise

For Every Season:
Daily Devotions

"I'm Going On
a Diet Tomorrow"

Marriage
Connections

Are We Living
in the Last Days?

"I'm Going On
a Diet Tomorrow"

Visit:

www.kerygmapublishing.com
www.allendavidbooks.com
www.harvest.org